GARDEN SONGS

A Spiritual Formation Field Journal

Cheryl Velk

CHERYL VELK

Garden Songs: A Spiritual Formation Field Journal
Copyright © 2020 by Cheryl Velk

ISBN 978-1-7345594-0-8 (paperback)
ISBN 978-1-7345594-1-5 (e-book)

Scripture quotations taken from the New American Standard Bible® (NASB),
Copyright © 1960, 1962, 1963, 1968, 1971, 1972, 1973, 1975, 1977, 1995 by
The Lockman Foundation. Used by permission. www.Lockman.org

Scripture taken from the Holy Bible, NEW INTERNATIONAL VERSION®,
NIV® Copyright © 1973, 1978, 1984, 2011 by Biblica, Inc.® Used by
permission. All rights reserved worldwide.

Cover design by Kelly Korak
Production Artist: Casey Bowser
Cover art by Cheryl Velk

This is for fellow members of the
Long Road and Hard Answers Club.

For daughters and sons living in exile
and longing to come home.

For anyone who has reached the
clearing and is listening.

For anyone whose ear is pressed
against the wall of faith.

You are loved, and you're not alone.

CONTENTS

VOICE

What is in me to express
that won't just add to
the noise, to the rage
to the whys, to the cries
to the self-satisfied lies
of what I perceive myself to be

The truth of me
is truth found in you, Lord
All that was unmet, unkept
I found in you
and so I will lift my praise
and all that could not raise
from my soul is released and
spiritual war is waged

and I find my voice
and your light shines through
and all touched by your grace
is made beautiful

CHERYL VELK

PROLOGUE

These are songs sung in gardens. In Eden and exile. In Gethsemane and other lonely places. Steps away from Golgotha at both morning and noon. And from the edges of paradise, following the sound of rustling leaves from the tree of life.

These are songs of celebration and lamentation. Perseverance and rest. Lostness and foundness. Helplessness and help.

I could tell a little more of my story, but this is more the story of the One whose story I've found myself within.

This book is a song of gratitude. A sacrifice of praise. A tithe of journaled days.

•

What I tell you in the darkness, speak in the light; and what you hear whispered in your ear, proclaim upon the housetops. ~Jesus (Matt. 10:27 NASB)

CHERYL VELK

EDEN

Now the Lord God had
planted a garden
in the east, in Eden;
and there he put
the man he had formed.
(Gen. 2:8 NIV)

CHERYL VELK

chapter one

INNOCENCE + EXILE

CASTAWAYS

my grandfather reading
Swiss Family Robinson to me
somehow the same chapter
each vacation
each visit
not so much the story as
the sharing of the story
shipwrecked on an island
together

on my borrowed bed
in the room my uncle sailed from
old lamplight like hot tea and honey
hovering near paintings of distant ports
and the black, carved wood of that
haunted Spanish wardrobe that
swallowed linens and children
while floorboards creaked with the
restlessness of midnight
like a ship cradled by waves

Cap'n Crunch waiting in the
morning like treasure
in Blue Willow bowls

LIGHT + SHADOWS

Summer sidewalk concrete too hot for five-year-old feet but shoes too constricting for my five-year-old heart, I stilled my dancing for split-second relief to tip the water pitcher beside a purple flower whose name I was still learning. Then the fidgety dance resumed as I listened to the whisper of the earth as it drank, its colors richening, before I took a step to the left to the next wonders to pour and watch and listen.

A few more steps down the path, and it was time to refill the pitcher half as big as me in the kitchen sink. Though I ran there and back, the earth was already pale and dusty again, as thirsty as ever under the Midwestern sun.

Still I poured and listened and ran to the sink and back again and again. Until every flower had a long sip.

Sweat making long, blonde hair and clothes cling to skin, I collapsed on the couch then. Unsettled. What had those whispers said? Those fragile flowers, their thirst ran deeper than the earth. I knew my best hadn't been enough to satisfy and yet here they lived.

Tears had dried over the miles in the green and white striped 1970s van as we'd made our way here. Driving away from our California home, our whole world waving, I'd sobbed in a panic, "No! Go back! Please, go back!" I hadn't realized until then the finality of all the packing. Not yet cried out, I'd gone silent as the "no, we can't" sank in. Tears enough to fill the ocean between us ran and fell, and ran and fell.

Back now where I'd been born, where my grandparents lived and all the stories before my own began their reverse-motion peek into the past, it was brief respite on our way even further east of my Eden to our new home. For the first time, this anchoring place we often visited felt a little foreign, but the only thing that had changed was me. My eyes were new, and I was noticing and asking different things.

Uneasy as we exchanged hugs at the end of our short visit, I climbed back into the van and buckled myself in. This was my last taste of the familiar. The key turned in the ignition, and we headed in a direction I'd never been before.

After a couple more days of driving, we stopped an hour or so shy of another ocean's beach. It seemed abrupt and random. Why here, of all places? Nothing could have been more different. Gone were the bright, panoramic views with nothing blocking horizon lines. Here was a densely packed maze filled with shadows, changing light, and hidden things.

Over the following weeks I rolled down windows, and my hand cupped hot, humid air like river water as we drove down narrow, tree-canopied streets. Staring into trees tightly spaced and knotted together with wild foliage straight out of the darker parts of a fairy tale, I felt both scared and brave and a pull toward the bigness of the story it was all telling. I was drawn to things that brushed its edges and hinted at its shape.

Those lush, dark green tunnels broke open into an assortment of scenes. Like farmland where we pulled over to roadside stands to buy corncobs still wrapped in their soft silk and wild, curling leaves. And like more populated stretches lined with homes from a bygone era. Some held fireplaces big enough for a kid to walk straight into fully upright, head bowed just a little.

Some roads gave way to rushing waters and to bridges built with stone and wood and hands. We heard the waters would rise there and overcome them, but they were still standing.

For a full day's drive in any direction, markers everywhere said that battles of one sort or another had been fought and things lost and won here.

Thin gravestones, pocked and fading, tilted with time just beyond the wrought iron railings that my fingers played against as we walked down sidewalks in town. New playmates I'd gotten closer to as weeks went by and school began taught me their game, and I, like they, held my breath while passing every grave.

Our neighborhood had no markers, no monuments, though. So new it was strange. Simple squares of the barest land tucked away in the middle of miles of forests and fields, awaiting seeds and sweat, creativity and rain. The blankest of blank slates. Why would they have done this, I remember thinking. Couldn't they have left something to start with?

But then my brother, four years older than me, ran upstairs one day, opening his hand to reveal a few arrowheads he'd just been given. Broken, old, and small—so ordinary, really—it took me a minute to recognize them as weapons. Things that could hurt or kill. He said ones just like them could probably be found right in our yard. Because all those stories from school, they'd happened right here.

He rushed off to search our earth for signs of a hunt or a fight, and that familiar tangled-forest feeling rose up in me from somewhere deep. And I knew right there in my bedroom with its butterscotch yellow walls and tiger-stripe maple chest, with its drawing paper and books and record albums, that there was nowhere that story didn't reach. And that the whole wide world, marked or otherwise, was a battlefield. From the beginning of time until now. Some battles we talk about, and some we don't.

•

My first prayer was a song.

In California I remember listening in pajamas from the upstairs banister to guitars and voices singing love songs below. My earliest years spent in the Jesus Movement's epicenter, in some of its own earliest years, I didn't quite get who Jesus was, but I was getting my first potent tastes of what real joy, peace, and love looked, felt, and sounded like. Strange then, that that wasn't where it clicked for me.

This new church in New Jersey held Sunday school in a gym. It was filled with rows of metal folding chairs that we'd move into clusters when it was time for our age-grouped lessons. I'd never seen a felt board before or heard about the paper people in robes who would stick to them. So odd, I didn't get it. But I listened to the stories and filed it all, more or less.

Kindergarten through twelfth grade, though, we all started out together in those rows. The red-headed man in the brown suit and tie would wave his arm high like we were a choir while a woman in nylons and pumps went to town playing on the upright piano. And when it came time to pray, he didn't like to stop. His eyes clenched shut, he meant what he was saying. Despite our impatience to get on with the fun stuff, for some reason that always seemed like his favorite thing.

For me that was the music. Here I was more in my element. And I recognized some of those same exact love songs and now got to join my voice to them. I still didn't understand them but liked to sing. To Johnny Cash or Joni Mitchell or John Newton, it didn't much matter, I just sang. Maybe that's why Grandma would always call me her chickadee.

But one Sunday as we rose and started to sing, grown-ups walked off to the side to the right and opened the double doors to the cool morning breeze and all that green. And a pillar of light no one else seemed to see walked right in. It moved to the front of the room and stopped.

I realize this part sounds very woo. Maybe that's why it took me so many years to find the language to even say it out loud. All I can say is that's what I saw.

And that's when I heard the words we were singing and, like finally finding the right key, everything opened, and I knew who it was and where all those felt-board figures were pointing. "Into My Heart," the song was called. A longing set to music, asking Jesus to come make his home in me and stay forever.

Stay. Please stay.

These were no magic words. I'd sung them before without a thing changing. Something else was at work now that made them a prayer. And what else can you do when you suddenly come alive but sing as loud as you can?

Prayers of invitation, altar calls—you won't find those exact things in the Bible. I mean, three thousand baptized in one day seems a lot like both when I picture that playing out, but at least not how we tend to go about it today. And, while many in Bible times were baptized with water on the spot, the thief on the cross next to Jesus could only say, "Remember me."

Many I've known don't even remember the one specific moment they set out following Jesus, the memory now merged with each footstep since then speaking another yes, and another.

But I'd heard verses saying how God, through his Holy Spirit, wants to dwell in us. In the seat of our own soul—a place where our will lives, not just our emotions or intellect. Our heart, for lack of a better way to put it. The driving part of us. And when my eyes were opened to him that morning, everything in me responded with an overwhelming yes. And I'll always be grateful for the song that helped me give voice to that and gave me a few words to start with.

> For this reason I kneel before the Father...I pray that out of his glorious riches he may strengthen you with power through his Spirit in your inner being, so that Christ may dwell in your hearts through faith. And I pray that you, being rooted and established in love, may have power, together with all the Lord's holy people, to grasp how wide and long and high and deep is the love of Christ, and to know this love that surpasses knowledge—that you may be filled to the measure of all the fullness of God. (Eph. 3:14,16-19 NIV)

I'd never understood a song better or meant it more, despite the mystery. Because it wasn't like answering a What, it was meeting a Who. I'd never sung to someone before. But that morning I did, with all my heart.

Afterwards I ran across the church to the back of the sanctuary to find my mother and told her, "I sang Jesus into my heart today."

It wasn't until we were out in the parking lot and getting into the van that she realized what I'd been trying to tell her. I had a couple "now let me get this straight..." theological questions as I was freshly processing all that I'd picked up but was just now learning. But I knew that I'd been changed. Too much made sense now for what I didn't yet know to get in the way.

•

Born into a broken world and reborn into all things being made new. But brokenness surrounded me, and in time I found that I, too, was broken and in need of remaking.

Why did this joy I couldn't shake and this embrace still come with this exile? Why didn't "In the beginning..." end neatly and quickly with "and they lived happily ever after" like all the other books, like all the other stories?

When did I start hiding? And why did I have to try so hard to keep our days from exploding?

It wasn't supposed to be this way.

Our square of earth turned a busy green, full of crabgrass and dandelions that turned to brown circles, poisoned. Lightning bugs floated overhead, and woolly bears made their way below. We ran there through sprinklers, through rain, through darkness, through daylight. We ran from, we ran to.

The trees along the side of the land wouldn't grow. Maybe it was the shouting. But our vegetable garden in back was a hundred square feet and full of rocks and feasts. Arms grew strong and knees grew weak.

This life isn't going to be easy.

Born in exile with the aroma of Eden still clinging to our memories' clothes, we come to our knees in a garden. And our labor becomes a prayer: Jesus, meet me here.

•

John 3:1-21, John 8:12, Acts 2:41, Rom. 8:9, Rom. 10:8-10, 1 Cor. 6:19, 1 Pet. 1:23

ILLUMINATED

the world a manuscript, illuminated
wild orange petals called me over
their collective shadow a letter C
drawn wildly but distinct
they beamed and, in part, said my name
I leaned in close, and lingered with them, shining
our shadows, together, spelling something
I hadn't the vantage point to see

HIDING

I'm hiding in your garden
in the cool of the day
I'm hiding from your eyes
as I hear you calling my name

there's a break in your voice
saying, "where have you gone"

I'm here, Lord
right here
but uncovered

I can't take it back
It's been done

I'm sorry
I'm sorry
I'm sorry

•

Gen. 3:8-9

EYES OPEN

Now and then I'll hear someone say that if you don't read every part of the Bible looking through the lens of love, you're going to miss the deeper meaning. But one day that landed particularly hard, and I challenged it. And my mind went straight to Eden because why beat around the hiding bush. Okay, Lord, what about the Fall? What about the curses? What about the wrath and heavy-duty consequences from one broken rule?

Just one. Can you imagine a world with just one rule? It's hard to go a day without breaking a few, and that's with me caring. But at the start there was just one. You have the best of everything else, just avoid this one thing: the tree of the knowledge of good and evil. You don't know what you'd be getting yourself into. At its heart, the smallest possible test of wills and trust.

God took us from one to ten to Leviticus, and then all the way back to two:

> Jesus replied: "'Love the Lord your God with all your heart and with all your soul and with all your mind.' This is the first and greatest commandment. And the second is like it: 'Love your neighbor as yourself.' All the Law and the Prophets hang on these two commandments." (Matt. 22:37-40 NIV)

Meanwhile, here and now our eyes continue to open to evil. Our eyes can't shut tight enough to keep us from seeing the lines we keep crossing. We turn away from the news, wishing we could unknow horrors we didn't know existed yesterday. And all our own laws, enough to fill libraries, haven't stopped evil from happening. It always finds an avenue.

What broke wasn't just a rule; it was unity. And isn't that the way it continues.

There's no place where God is not, but Eden was that place of extravagant provision and blessing rooted in intimacy. And, despite it all, they still found themselves questioning whether they might be better off without him. Even in heaven, the question had already spread like a virus and, well, that escalated quickly. I shake my head thinking "I'd never" until I remember my own independent streak. I, too, am prone to holding back corners of my life from anyone's say-so or eyes, even God's.

Not sure I see any way around the question we're each bound to consider at some point, in some way, explicitly stated or not. And, the thing is, he never wanted slaves. This exile, this separation, would begin his own search for his true sons and daughters. Those who want not just what he has, but who he is.

Still, I had to ask.

Yes, God lost no time covering us; it was the first thing he did. Yes, he lost no time fighting for us and making a way of reconciliation that would cost him everything. Yes, he made a way of grace for those who'll take it and that all started right here. There wasn't the slightest hesitation. He'd known that by offering us choice and freedom this would happen.

What I really wanted to know: In that moment, what was the sound of his voice and the look in his eyes?

Almost before my question finished taking shape, God reading my heartache, a few lines sprang to mind. Those same ones proclaimed, debated, and pondered by princes, paupers, saints, mockers, and me. And shouted once in a while by preachers of the angrier variety.

> To the woman he said, "I will make your pains in childbearing very severe; with painful labor you will give birth to children…" (Gen. 3:16 NIV)

> To Adam he said, "…Cursed is the ground because of you; through painful toil you will eat food from it all the days of your life. It will produce thorns and thistles for you, and you will eat the plants of the field. By the sweat of your brow you will eat your food until you return to the ground…" (Gen. 3:17-19 NIV)

But this time, instead of flinching, I breathed. There, hiding in plain sight, God's own heart beats and breaks and grieves.

•

I'd waited until a month before the due date to buy them a gift. My first act of faith after eight months of holding my breath and avoiding eye contact with both God and myself. They'd had two miscarriages before— dare I hope this time? This baby wasn't mine but was the first of this new generation of our family, and all of us were still guarding our hopes so carefully. Too cautious to celebrate too freely. Not before seeing that child with our own eyes.

I was there to buy a baby carrier. So I could somehow help these parents hold this little one close to their hearts. But how could I trust that their arms would not be left empty?

Halfway through the store the levee breached, and I couldn't stop crying.

When I got home, it was like a tidal wave. Hitting my hands and knees, a wail from the depths of me erupted, driven by the force of my heart's tectonic plates fully shifting to a new place. My lungs and throat too small a passageway, the cry was equal parts whisper and scream: "God, I don't want to be angry with you!" And then came tumbling out, in crashing waves, all those emotions and words that had been weighing so heavily. Anger, grief, confusion, sorrow.

I'd been so numb about the subject for the whole pregnancy. But now every word, every question, every fear—so many unspoken even to myself as I'd left them sitting there alone in the dark—all came rushing out at God's feet. Cracked wide open, they were all escaping. Lament of the old-school kind, only ashes and torn clothes were missing.

And somewhere in the middle of all that, I noticed how he was listening. I wasn't alone. There was intimacy. And instead of a satisfied vengeance, or even just patiently waiting me out, there he was, it seemed, so present, with tears of his own and saying, "I know. I know."

•

Pain. People smarter than me have been struggling with this since the beginning of time. Is God really good? Can he be trusted? Why was this ever allowed? Why, God? Why?

Loss, tragedy—none of this was the type of pain he'd been talking about in the garden that day. That different subject is neither tidy nor tame and the case-by-case answers go well above my pay grade. It would be cruel and inaccurate to conflate it all into one blanket statement. It's just that in that place I caught a glimpse of God's face. Even within this situation and my more peripheral position in it—things he hadn't directly meant in that moment.

That verse about the pain of childbirth. What if it was never about pain being doled out for the sake of itself, but about pain radiating? Reflecting the cost of what went missing and the magnitude of the price God had immediately promised to pay.

> "'For in him we live and move and have our being.' As some of your own poets have said, 'We are his offspring.'" (Acts 17:28 NIV)

If in him we live and move and exist, how could pain—either ours or his—be fully containable? Exclusive to any of us. Though even now it's hard for me to grasp the gravity, I'm struck by these pictures of what had been lost with that first act of stepping away. And with all of our stepping away.

That there would be increased pain in childbirth—isn't that what God had just committed himself to? A cost so high to our promised rebirth, though to him it was somehow worth it.

And that there would be labor, that we would struggle and experience futility—isn't that what God himself had just entered into? Laboring to reconcile his creation to himself, knowing multitudes would reject him even after all of that.

Even in these darkest words, there was an invitation. Would we try understanding what we'd done with all our choosing everything and everyone other than our Maker? Would we be willing not just to be rescued but to join in his own labor and longing and identify with his heart?

•

Because of Jesus, futility and pain will not have the last words.

> Christ redeemed us from the curse of the Law, having become a curse for us—for it is written, "CURSED IS EVERYONE WHO HANGS ON A TREE"—in order that in Christ Jesus the blessing of Abraham might come to the Gentiles, so that we would receive the promise of the Spirit through faith. (Gal. 3:13-14 NASB)

An incomparable gift incomparably paid for, transforming at the most foundational level through no strength or merit of our own when we embrace it. Indwelled by the Holy Spirit, reconciliation with Almighty God our Father accomplished.

Yet all it takes is one look within and around us to know that all is not yet as it should be. And one quick Scripture word search on endurance to know it won't fully be until heaven. We still live on this battleground even though the larger war has already been won. We're promised, though, that one day all the combat within and around us will stop. One day God will say, "Enough." Until then we take one step forward, and then another. But together—no small thing.

This child we'd waited nine long months for did make it. As did another after still more loss and waiting and fighting. Their births just the beginning of another kind of labor. How can your heart sit idly by in the face of so much growing and learning? From first steps to first choices, they have such an invested cheering section.

God help me say this, I'm on such tender ground.

I've never carried a child, but I've seen enough to know that infinite factors go into each individual birth experience. Among all my loved ones who've become mothers, I've yet to witness perfect repetition of any one story or any one set of thoughts and emotions. And I get that no list will ever be long enough to include the nuances or even broad strokes of all the other stories out there.

But more than once I've witnessed a new mother in a moment when her eyes have locked with the eyes of the life that came forth from her. The life that now needs and trusts her and hangs on her every word. And more than once in such a moment I've seen a mother smiling through tears. The complexity of thought and emotion too personal, too intimate to pinpoint, the commonality only the profound sense of bigness. And a sensory memory comes to me, even now, of my whole spirit resting against God's heart. Feeling the vibration in that chest accompanying the quiet voice in my ears.

And that's the image that made me wonder if the birth of a child might be a little closer to what that celebration in heaven is like when one of God's longed-for, labored-for children turns to him. Something intensely complex and personal happening while angels and saints like friends and family erupt with joy and laughter at the news.

This is by no means to say that I grasp it all. The hows and whys of everyone hitting different points on the spectrum of ease or toil, enjoyment or suffering, or loss or gain. The mysteries and intricacies of the disparities. That's more complex and goes beyond this conversation. I only know there's a measure of labor and pain none of us is immune to. Not just mothers. Not just farmers. And I've come to know God's unfathomable joy in redeeming.

> For we know that the whole creation groans and suffers the pains of childbirth together until now. And not only this, but also we ourselves, having the first fruits of the Spirit, even we ourselves groan within ourselves, waiting eagerly for our adoption as sons, the redemption of our body. For in hope we have been saved, but hope that is seen is not hope; for who hopes for what he already sees? But if we hope for what we do not see, with perseverance we wait eagerly for it. (Rom. 8:22-25 NASB)

God's heart is reflected in all of it. He relates. There's both joy and pain for him in our birth. He grieves—his heart the first to ever break—and he celebrates. He knows every name.

He knows. He knows.

•

Gen. 3:8-24, Luke 15:4-10, John 16:21-22, Acts 17:22-34, Rom. 8:18-25, Rev. 21:4-7, Rev. 22:1-4

COMPLEXITY + SIMPLICITY

here at the end of such a day
how is one to hold this complexity
in a simple way
maybe in the act of
setting all this before you, Lord
for you to hold for me
while I search for your face
for your heart
for what you would say to me

GETHSEMANE

Jesus went out as usual
to the Mount of Olives,
and his disciples followed him.
(Luke 22:39 NIV)

CHERYL VELK

chapter two

A LONELY PLACE

CONSTELLATIONS

Lord, we search your works like
blind fingers touching a face
and, crying out, we listen
for echoes of your grace
but here I am again
trying to find a place where
we haven't yet obscured
every glorious last trace

I went out to listen
to the chorus of the earth
but couldn't hear your praises
over engines racing
I went to find horizon
through the maze of what we've made
and I went to find the stars
but drones danced in the way

I want to see your glory, Lord
tonight I need this glimpse of you
but they can't even leave
the constellations alone

•

Rom. 1:20

CANYONS + COLORS

Prayer closets. Corners. Rooms with closed doors. The places to spend time with God that I grew up hearing about in church, they always sounded like they were supposed to be small. And the smaller the better.

I still remember childhood Sunday school classes, listening to the conversation shift into a bit of a verbal hide-and-seek contest—the winner, the one who could think of the tiniest, darkest hiding place in their home. By the end of those classes I was nearly gasping for air.

They had a way of making even our inner chamber, that most private place in our homes—and in us—sound small, the way they'd talk about it in solemn tones.

Jesus even used some of those words. They'd quote him. And my own bedroom, door closed, was my favorite place to read my Bible and talk to him. I knew what he'd meant, despite the one-upping over it. But I'd also read this:

> But Jesus often withdrew to lonely places and prayed.
> (Luke 5:16 NIV)

Lonely places. The wilderness, some versions translate it. No one as far as the eye could see.

Wouldn't that be something nowadays? Traffic and schedules the way they are, such settings now strike mental images of travel magazine photo shoots and vacation-type getaways. Retreat centers, campgrounds, and homes on hills. Or a five-dollar cup of coffee somewhere with an amazing view. But some friends with toddlers would settle for five minutes of privacy to even just take a shower. While others can't stop working hard to put food on the table, and to them these types of havens and breaks are luxuries.

The truth is, if you live in the right part of town or have enough money, your eyes most likely will be a little less heavy.

The rare chance to get away from towns full of man-made lights and find a cloudless sky full of stars, that's medicine to me. Still more so if it comes with nature's loud silence, pure and undisturbed. But with one former home it took a two-hour drive before you'd stop seeing signs and power lines, and even then, cars never stopped rushing by.

Find beauty, get away, wherever you can, but the point is the Father. The point is intimacy and recalibration of spirit and attention. There are things we need that we can't buy, and they happen in places—both big and small—that don't take money to find.

The other thing I've always heard our daily time with God should be: quiet. "Be sure to have your quiet time with God."

Father, thank you for the Psalms.

What a gift that we get to read and study the Bible, God's inspired Word. We need to quiet ourselves and listen. Really listen. But in the wilderness there's also freedom to shout and wrestle and sing—all of it versions of intimacy. It's a place where two fully present hearts meet.

•

Try to describe a sunrise.

Did you do it justice?

Friends have heard my best attempts at describing life these days, but it's just God and me in this room as I stare out these windows, listen to this silence, and write these words. I can try to lead people to this spot, but it stays just out of reach. They can't see the colors I'm seeing.

There is terrain that only God and I can walk together. The terrain of the heart. The best I can do is offer grainy snapshots so much less than life size and wish they'd been there.

Even in a crowd, every breath between spoken phrases is wind blowing across my own Grand Canyon, and that view and my heart's shifting colors over it will never be shared or witnessed by anyone other than God. This is my lonely place where I go daily to talk to my Father. To sing, to cry, to listen, to laugh, to fast, to be comforted, to persevere, to long, to dream, to remember, to build altars and hope the sacrifices there release an aroma God loves.

My lonely place. Vast. It's not a corner or a closet, it's a world. Father, this is where I seek you. Meet me here.

All day yesterday there was a feeling I couldn't quite give words to. Stopping there, I finally asked myself, "Where are you in your lonely place right now?" Somehow, picturing the specific landscape brought both clarity and comfort. Not in a visualization way but with our artist God's own language of metaphor—his green pastures, his quiet waters—helping me say what needed saying. Asking that question in church as the music began, I then sang to God from that territory, singing out to him over my lonely place.

Where am I? In a canyon between two cliffs. In a desert, thirsty. Knee deep in a fast river. In a churning sea, holding onto the Rock for the life of me.

Lead me from there to green pastures. Lead me from there to quiet waters. I don't know the way; please lead me.

Our true lonely places are vast. Stretching from horizon to horizon. Big enough to get lost in and to need God's help finding our way back. Big enough to empty ourselves into and, inhaling, receive. His breath still our life.

We do need to get away with our Father. Intentional, set aside moments and minutes and hours. But with space shrinking around us daily, we begin with the lonely place we don't need to get away to find.

•

Ps. 23, Ps. 51:16-17, Matt. 6:6, Mark 1:45, Mark 6:31

IN THE CLEARING

in the clearing
in the quiet
strange beating

wings, heart
things troubled by stillness
and taking flight

but with no destination
save this clearing
this quiet

so troubled beating breathes
resisting itself
to stop and listen

still feeling the forest
and searching the far-off shadows
lest a dark dream take heed

a dare of a note calls it out
nothing comes but echo upon echo fading

all this beating...

how could even frightened birds
have been made
for anything but singing

SCAFFOLDING

People have been there for me this past week, but not in the way I've needed them. While the two replies I got today helped, there was a place in me their words didn't reach.

How can that place feel so hidden when it's all around and within me? How could a person miss a target that big?

It's one thing to seek out a lonely place. It's another thing entirely for it to come looking for you.

If a single person admits to loneliness, there's that risk of pity or judgment. And if someone who has someone admits to loneliness, will someone judge their choice of mate?

Or are these our own private questions, usually left unspoken because it's proven unsafe? Maybe that's what prompts the abrupt dismissiveness, or so many smug or relieved responses in both directions of "See?" when someone takes one for the team and risks some vulnerability.

"Just serve and don't think about it and you won't feel that way" has its limits at the end of the day. Just like "what right do you have to be lonely" has its limits when you're sitting across the dinner table from eyes that don't always fully see you.

Some of the loneliest people I've ever known are married, and some of the most sacrificial people I've ever known are single or childless. How did this become a contest of needs, benefits, or wholeness? Calling each other's differing consolations selfishness doesn't help matters any. We could have that debate all day. Let's not.

What if we began to give space to hear what each other's saying? Instead of growing the distance between us, the vastness of our lonely places unnecessarily increasing.

What if loneliness doesn't always mean a mistake? What if it just speaks to our human state?

I've yet to meet even a particularly charmed life that's one hundred percent spared from loneliness. From that empty space. Though we can get pretty good at avoiding this territory. Through more or through less. Staying busy or numbing out. Filling our minds and time to overflowing with other things, or just not thinking. One way or another, diverting our attention or drowning the longing out.

The pros among us end up decorating the avoidance in gold leaf. I'm doing this—work, ministry, this never, ever stopping—for the most admirable reasons. What's the point in asking questions or feeling or even just stopping to breathe? Isn't that for the weak?

All this that looks like strength can become our shoring. Supporting beams we keep adding where we're meant to be free-standing. All this that looks like strength can become our scaffolding. Hiding, with the buzz of our exterior work, a foundation needing testing.

•

Even in Eden with God's undivided attention and physical presence, there was a type of relational need that he wanted us to meet for each other. When one became two then became one again together, the word "helper" was the same word later used for the Holy Spirit. One of God's own names. The marriage relationship, that picture of Jesus Christ and his church, his bride. The first human relationship, and the only one that tasted life before the fall. Holy.

But then others came along exponentially, and community involved another holy picture: Christ's body, of which each child of God is a part and Jesus is the head.

When did we begin to separate and alienate what was meant not just to be one flesh but one body? All of us fully functioning in unity. Not just spouses and parents and children but brothers and sisters.

At a former church, I sat among young families for years feeling phantom limb pain for all who were missing—those without kids or mates—while they assumed my frustrations in certain moments and conversations were all for the sake of the ring that was not on my left hand. What I was actually saying was too big of a disconnect.

Why are you still here, they'd sometimes probe aloud in ways both subtle and direct, and not a couple towns over where we've heard there's a place for your people? Why didn't you leave like the others who came and went long ago, finding nothing here for them?

Because if I left, the divide would have been just that much bigger, and the thought of it broke my heart. Because I don't want to be segregated. Because I love my married friends. Because it doesn't define me to that extent. Because it's not the primary thing I look for in a church.

Whenever I tried to broach the subject of the imbalance, the emphatic answer was always the same—that it was critical for families to know they had support there. As if the rest of the surrounding community didn't need that every bit as much? As if I didn't? Never mind that every other church I'd visited had the same emphasis. The same biases. The same assumptions.

I wasn't looking for programs tailored to me, just a broadened conversation. But even that seemed to be received as a threat to the mission of the church. And their minds would still go to an adolescent youth group formula for midlifers, retirees, and widows, so they'd know how to advertise their openness. They'd think and sometimes say, "Why doesn't she start it herself?" Wanting nothing to do with it, themselves.

Trust me, we don't want that, either. Not what you're picturing, not like that. More than anything, we just really want a seat at the table. Across from you. Not at the kiddie table, set apart even within the same room. Not as a tool or a project or a program, but family.

Meanwhile, I began to hear diverse reasons that others even within demographics of focus also felt like a social exception. People I'd assumed were on the inside track. Our divisions aren't just about family or the lack thereof. Not even close. We're more complex than that.

Many of our cultural divides are deep and wide, and it takes a lot to cross them in a meaningful way. For everyone. But maybe we're overcomplicating it a little. Small things can go a long way. Small moments built upon. Two-way conversations. Suspension of assumptions. Insightful questions. Deep listening. Rather than a desire to make someone feel heard, a desire to actually hear.

For years, in our "Complexity Level: Bumper Sticker" encouragement kind of way, I'd always heard the first two lines of Psalm 68:6 (NASB), and usually just the first:

God makes a home for the lonely;
He leads out the prisoners into prosperity…

People always left off the last line, and so even with my own reading it took me years to even notice:

…Only the rebellious dwell in a parched land.

It's not just everybody else. Something's required of each of us as it relates to stepping into community. Whether it's setting down pride or comfort zone or an unhelpful identity. Our what-I-am has become our who-I-am—our title, our personality type, our tax bracket, our marital status, our children's ages or existence, our race, our accent, our wounds, our strengths, our ballot choices, our intellect, our disabilities, our fitness, our giftings, our style choices, our looks, our obsessions, our age and generation—and we end up looking no different than the culture we come from. Worshiping the same idols and looking to the same things as the world for acceptance and meaning and safety and purpose. Finding others most like us and calling that community.

Maybe it is for us, but is it really when some find they have to move on when their circumstances change a bit, or when the questions they start asking rock the boat a little? Or when others walk in the door and walk right back out, sensing the unspoken acceptance criteria? Telling more than showing when it comes to Jesus. God, forgive us.

> For them I sanctify myself, that they too may be truly sanctified. My prayer is not for them alone. I pray also for those who will believe in me through their message, that all of them may be one, Father, just as you are in me and I am in you. May they also be in us so that the world may believe that you have sent me. (John 17:19-21 NIV)

Unity, so that the world might see a picture of Jesus bigger than our own individual stories. Those are crucial, too, but our true who-I-am is family, all children of the King, and our divisions leave us all on the outside looking in or not quite knowing where to start when it comes to community. Sometimes it's you, sometimes it's me. We are living smaller stories than intended.

Maybe one part of the "you have to be like a child to enter the kingdom" thing is about how before a certain age kids see beyond every possible difference and are just accepting and curious. In seconds a total stranger becomes a best friend, and we stand by with tears in our eyes as we witness the holiness of the bridges they build among us again.

To be a child again seems like the most impossible request. Like being born again or squeezing through the eye of a needle. God, accomplish this in us.

This isn't about niceness or one more fleeting human attempt at utopia. What we offer each other is something forged and nurtured in private, one-on-one with God and by the power of his Spirit. How else can we be Jesus' hands and feet? Part of his own body? How else could we possibly do what he's asking?

Our lonely places are so much bigger than they need be. And there's a lot we can and should do to shrink them. At the same time, there remains something in every single one of us that can only be truly satisfied in God. Something we can't self-generate. And trying to get it from others or from grand plans or from our own wisdom and strength leads to frustration.

But we try. Oh, do we ever try. And sometimes it's only after we've exhausted all our trying or our beams and planks give way that we come to the clearing, to the quiet. To our lonely place. Away from our fixes, our distractions, our preoccupations. And once in a hard while, even away from our purest blessings and our loving investments of time and attention. Willing to hear something new about ourselves. Willing to face both the knowns and unknowns of what needs facing.

•

Jesus himself needed others in different ways at different times. None so rawly as his last night in Gethsemane when, in their confusion and exhaustion and grief, all his friends could do was sleep. He kept asking them to stay awake—stay, please stay—but they couldn't. But because he'd come to that same garden often, despite all that was missing that night he had the depth of relationship with his Father to move forward with strength.

It can be life changing to surrender to God who or what, in a perfect world, should be there but isn't. Just as it can be life changing to recognize and challenge our shoring and scaffolding—who or what we've relied on or pursued or focused on more than God. Maybe even in his name.

What have we been leaning on because we've intellectually believed but essentially doubted our framework would hold? Even the one most worthy of our trust, God himself, can be experienced as a weak thing in our lives, for all practical purposes, if he's hidden behind our shoring. What would it be like to take God at his word and find ourselves strengthened or filled up or moved forward in a way not our doing?

And what would it be like for more and more of us to come to each other out of that place?

There are stretches of our lonely place we don't readily go. Those places of not just comfort and companionship but of getting to the stripped-down truth of ourselves. It takes courage to face head-on the ground we're not used to covering, and without the voices we're used to hearing.

When other supports aren't there or come up insufficient, what it awakens in us is a longing to know God's enoughness. In such a moment, if by grace that longing's other names fall away and we see it for what it is, will we move toward God with all of this instead of keeping a safer distance? Will we test and taste what we say amen to? Will we seek a deeper amen?

Go there with hands empty. Go there with your clumsy not knowing what to say. Just go. He will meet you on the way, running.

•

Ps. 68:5-6, Matt. 18:2-4, Luke 15:20, John 14:15-16, John 14:26, John 15:26, John 16:7, Eph. 5:25-32

IMPOSSIBLE

Father, what do we ever
come to you for
if not the impossible

is anything at all with you
possible
yet here I am, with you
listening
Alpha, Omega, and me—
really?

to think that you pursue,
save, hear, cover, claim, change
we who fail
we who go our own way
we who, like you, cannot
will not
control what love does and
does not come our way…

our reconciliation
with you relies on
something so beyond us

I could say the same in the
face of the divides we live
so deep and wide
all despite knowing we're
already one in you
by definition

what is the deeper chasm
which alienation
which separation
the one between you and us

or between us and our
brothers and sisters

you bridged the one
the infinitely further crossing
impossible
uncrossable by us
what small thing for you
to do the latter

•

Matt. 19:26

THIS BODY

this body…
this tool
this habitation
this expression
this disguise

how can I rest in what
I fight
and what fights me
every minute

Father, it's you I rest in
within this body
within this friend
within this foe

how can even I alone
be one as you are one
without your unifying
compassion

you speak truces over me
and within me

•

John 17:20-21

CHERYL VELK

chapter three

PILGRIMAGE

LINES

the way the graphite sounded and felt
as I drew the pencil tip along the wall
lightly, hoping no one would notice, was
too exquisite to resist
better than paper
behind my pillow at the head
of the bed, making
small lines and swirls while
The Blue Danube played from
the music box hanging on the wall—
the one from my grandmother
who said this is where all the stories
before your own began
more or less

I pulled the plastic ball at the
end of the cord
and the song began again
and I was lost in the
butterscotch yellow wall
daring to make another line
of my own there
lightly

MOVING + STANDING STILL

Who was the one, I wonder, who gave my great-great-grandmother's family the surname that meant "to hope"? Who was the first one to choose that moniker? I still feel its pull from the other end of these connecting threads even though my own name came from the other side of the family. My dad even bought a vowel just before marrying, obscuring his surname's origins and meaning. Though legacies aren't sticklers for spelling.

Back when the oldest storytellers were still with us, every extended family visit would come with the same stories repeated over and over. Adding a new one or two of our own to the canon each time, we never minded the repetition. Just the opposite. Like a song you never tire of hearing, it was an oral storytelling tradition that went beyond mere information.

In seven short years, though, we lost half of our family—the entire remainder of that oldest generation, and one person far too young—and that tradition all but stopped. Connecting threads were broken and left hanging. Stories spooled to the floor like ribbon as hands let go and the lines went slack.

It was the arrival of a new generation that turned my recurring tug into a compulsion. In my own way of fighting for family, I went back to where those lines had fallen and began the painstaking work of putting them in order. Tending to them. Holding them gently and untangling each strand. Writing out the stories, jogging my own memory and others', and going beyond what even my grandparents had known, playing detective with our family history.

As more details emerged so did themes. And as more answers came so did brand new questions. Like wondering about the story behind that hope-filled name. And like what to make of my own line in that tree. When I look close enough at the end of this line, this offshoot that's mine, there are dozens of strands intertwining that give it its particular texture and strength. I am both of it and something else. Curious.

One year later, there I was at the end of all of those threads once again pulled taut. Not for a second believing that the story itself was wrapping up, it called the question of my place in it all. The story pulsing from the other end and asking me to walk forward was so big. And I felt so small.

Maybe it was growing up hearing all the old country and coming-to-America tales that gave me this built-in assumption of the bigness of our individual stories and everything riding on them. Larger than life, they boldly stepped out.

As much as this cast of characters had never ceased to intrigue, entertain, and caution me, now I saw them together, stitched into this intricate design stretching out further than I could even get my head around. And certain patterns and themes now left me sensing the presence of a conductor or an architect. I'd found myself within a story so much bigger than my own, and my place in it felt both within and outside of my control. All at once I felt authored and born, inspired and mystified, responsible and helpless.

The questions written in letters the size of planets were what are you looking for, where are you looking, and why? And do you want it enough to go all in? The songs they moved through in orbit sounded like promises, though I couldn't make out the words.

The day the project was finally as finished as I could get it, I hugged the two-hundred-page notebook to myself. The weight felt greater than the physical pages, and my thoughts went to Abraham seeing all those stars and all those grains of sand. Jaw on the floor and forgetting how to blink, he must have asked, "Who am I?" Feeling small as a grain of sand himself but hearing that the story and promises he'd stepped into were as big as the sky.

Long after I gave copies of the project as Christmas presents, I continued to think about all the handwritten census pages and manifests from ships that landed at Ellis Island. And how I'd kept noticing these single adult women here and there living with their parents. Culturally a much different time, that type of arrangement wasn't quite as difficult for some to understand. Even as recently as a few years before my birth, my parents and brother had been part of a four-generation home.

Those women, theirs were among the stories I'd never been told. Because people usually care where the lines go, not where they stop. It makes sense that my eyes were drawn to them. They felt familiar.

Am I, like they, where the line frays? Or are we like rest notes in music to be read as a whole? Is the larger story we tell missing something?

This, of course, goes beyond singleness, this issue of childlessness. Especially nowadays many couples are in that same place. Some by choice, and some not. It's a larger question that's percolating in me about those lines that stop. The stories that don't always get heard or passed on, and what they might tell us if they did. Not about the empty place but about who or what did or didn't fill it.

We always heard that further back on my maternal grandmother's side the families were so huge that many siblings chose to have few or no children. But that's not enough to describe them. Had there been romance or loss? Was there contentment or sadness? Were any living with extended family out of necessity? Obligation? Expectation? Love? Were they quirky in a wonderful or yikes way? Were they lovely? Funny? Plain? Were they thinkers or feelers, both or neither? Fighters or peacemakers? Marthas or Marys? Were their lives vivid or as faded as that census ink?

I ask because I'm one of them. One of the rest notes in a magnum opus.

•

There are half a dozen states and one U.S. territory where I've lived that I suppose I can still call home. Illinois, California, New Jersey, Colorado, New Mexico, Hawaii, and Johnston Atoll. And then there are the states I spent time in nearly every summer, memories just as formative and vivid. And a handful of other states and countries, a few in particular, that feel so like me.

Then there's every place my feet have ever touched. A random diner here or there, a park or a bridge or a corner, the right song playing at the right moment transforming the most obscure coordinates into a place I belonged. And what about the place my whole family on all sides came from that I've never seen with my own eyes? And what about where I'm going? Nothing I can predict at this point.

I get flummoxed when someone asks where I'm from. As if it's still there, just waiting for me, specific and unchanged. It's easier to be asked where I am right now, this second. And the part of me that, right here, feels most awake.

When I left New Jersey for Colorado at sixteen I didn't let go any easier than I did in leaving California, though on the surface I did. That was the year home went from being something I was losing again to something I just didn't have. Even in those last months before moving, the place I belonged, the place I was from, suddenly felt like a phantom. Every place felt temporary now, and I began to use the word "home" more loosely.

It made sense to focus on the possibilities. The adventure. The exploring. And I didn't mind the chance to be new, at least in others' eyes. I kept moving, and change became one of the things I was best at.

For years my wanderings were about trying to find my place. The place where the life I was expected to have would finally kick in. As if I were a lock searching for its key as an answer to its reason for being. To truly, fully fit with another person or place or endeavor, maybe that would solve the riddle that I was to myself.

I tried following the generally accepted guidelines, then tried the opposite. Each left me throwing my hands up after a certain point.

It took about twenty moves, both local and distant, before work unexpectedly brought me back to Colorado. Right back to where my wanderings had started. And it crossed my mind that, despite all my growth and changes, there was a core, driving part of me so restless that still didn't feel any different. And it seemed like God was saying, "You might want to take a look at that."

I'd spent my life a nomad, trying different dwellings, cultures, careers, and adventures on for size. Each situation drawing out things that surprised me. For both better and worse, things I hadn't necessarily realized were in me. Life had moved forward, though forward felt like backward each time I dealt with the same old urge to start over.

I hadn't been to the end of the world but, like we used to say on that little atoll, you could see it from there. And that's where I finally understood that what I was looking for wasn't going to be found in a place, but in God.

It wasn't just a change of scenery I'd craved. I'd been looking for something a little like the right pair of shoes that I could wear for a full day without my feet hurting, only to discover it was my feet that needed a closer look.

Winding up back in Colorado of all places after all that was the last thing I'd expected. But it's where I finally stood still and the real pilgrimage began. Now I was finally really getting somewhere.

•

Father, both my stops and my starts challenge me. Those times you ask me to move and those times you ask me to stand still.

This movement isn't just about getting somewhere, is it. Nowhere with a GPS arrival flag, that is. No shrine, no relic, no monument. It was never about somewhere else. You're my destination. You. My latitude, my longitude, I've been moving both to and with you all this time. Learning your steps as you set the pace on this pilgrimage to see your face this side of someday.

And it's no straight line. The straight line I'd expected, hoped for, grieved not having. The answers I'd wanted clear and direct rather than woven into me stitch by winding stitch. It's meant moving forward and circling back. It's meant things that make little sense to me at the time but are often clearer in hindsight. At times I've fought your direction and ended up so lost and tangled up. And at times I've trusted you to lead and found myself in the sweetest dance.

This moving, this standing still, these patterns, these steps. These notes and rests. You and I like planets in a sky full of story, moving through promises like music, together.

•

Gen. 16:13, Ps. 139:9-10

BEYOND SUNSET

Sunset Road
my horizon line
there be dragons beyond
so you and your bicycle stay on this side

pedaling down side streets named
for the animals that used to linger here
handlebar tassels catching air
a costume jewelry necklace and a snack
in the woven, flowered basket

a small world
big enough to get lost in
traveling around it twice
in a morning

then home for apples
and PBJ
and a book from a place
far beyond Sunset

THIS WAITING PLACE

Cloud-surrounded by day
Burning with fire by night
Lord, dwell in these places
Bless me with your presence
Speak to me as a friend

When you say "go" I will go
When you say "stay" I will
stay in your embrace
within this desert place
this waiting space, your
womb that transforms me
You make all things new

Speak to me as a friend
Speak to me face to face

I can't see beyond this cloud
but you're in it and I know
when it moves I move with you
You promised to dwell in the cloud
and fill it with your presence
and lead me from here
I travel the long way with you

I can't feel beyond this fire
it threatens to consume but
it leaves the things you intended
while breezes find the ashes
of their bindings and carry them away
without my even noticing
'til one day the freedom dawns on me

Speak to me as a friend, Lord
Speak to me face to face

Within this cloud by day
Within this fire by night
This waiting, desert place
This womb

•

Exod. 13:21

A LAMP UNTO MY FEET

Some years back I had a dream where I was sitting beside one of those old, ornate lamps. The kind where you pull the little chain and three light bulbs go on and off in a different combination each time. Pull the chain once, and one bulb goes on. Pull the chain again, and that bulb goes off but two others go on. Pull it a third time, and one of those bulbs turns off and the other goes back on again. I kept pulling the chain, unsuccessfully trying to get all three bulbs to go on at the same time. Meanwhile, someone in the next room was looking for me. Someone who loved me.

Other details made it clear that the three bulbs within the one lamp represented the Trinity. And the idea was that whenever my theological, logical mind tried to understand the faces within the Godhead, one or two of them were perpetually left outside of my grasp at any given time. While this was effortless to roll with as a child, over time a certain oneness was lost.

> This, then, is how you should pray: "Our Father in Heaven..." (Matt. 6:9 NIV)

Don't pray to Jesus, I was often corrected. Don't have that conversation with him—it's God the Father we pray to. And the Holy Spirit is the one who indwells and helps us, distinctly unique from Jesus and Father God. The one Jesus left to send to us. My attention and conversation were continually directed and redirected toward God the Father and toward the Holy Spirit. And after a certain point, Jesus never quite fit into that conversational grid anymore. At least not naturally.

I knew Jesus remained active. So why did it feel like he had gone missing?

•

Great emphasis is given to God as Father, and rightly so. And to those verses that reveal ways God has a mother's heart and role, too. And then, of course, there's Jesus as bridegroom and the church his bride.

But it's less common to hear any real depth of attention given to the working out of Jesus as brother. Pointing out the shocking honor of it, yes, but not digging too far into the relational implications. Not really.

The Good Samaritan and Cain's defensive question are about as close as we get. When the challenge goes further, we do start to squirm a bit. In a weird way, strangers are easier. It's with those right in front of us regularly that deeper challenges tend to kick in. The church knows how to serve and does it exceedingly well, but there's a way of serving and doing community where we can retain our independence from each other. Am I the only one who's ever felt that it can take a crisis to be seen and supported? Or facilitated time put on the church calendar by others to have any sense of connection?

I don't mean that to sound like I'm not a part of the problem. We've all grown accustomed to our self-sustaining, fragmented units. Me, myself, and I have gotten pretty good at handling business. And while it's easy to feel overlooked and shut out by some, who am I missing in the process? I'm not immune from or above that. It costs to enter in.

My own brother lives twelve hundred miles away; relationship sweet but impacted understandably in both directions by life's demands and distance. Many can relate, while other friends have lost siblings to greater degrees to misunderstandings, to wildly differing goals or opinions, and to hurts, competition, and impasses. And still others to suicide, tragedy, and physical and mental illness.

Decades later many are left still trying to make sense of it. While the rest of us join them in feeling the empty space our brothers and sisters leave like a tooth gone that a tongue can't stop playing with. Our first friend, to one degree or another gone missing.

No one talks that much about sibling grief, or what someone's absence can do not just to parents or their children but to a sister or brother.

This is every bit as big as parent/child stuff. Maybe even more so, because we know our parents won't always be around but we expect our siblings to be. We came from the same place, so we, above all others, should remain each other's greatest champions, protectors, encouragers, and confidantes. Shouldn't we? But in this world, it often presents as varying degrees of absence.

Jesus, where did you go? You said you sent someone in your place—the Holy Spirit, our helper. But why don't you call? Why don't you visit? Or do you? Are you still here for me? Not just there, not just somewhere distant, but right here. Somehow. Some way. I miss your presence, face to face. Help me see you.

•

The picture God gave us of himself in his Son is such a gift.

> Jesus answered, "Don't you know me, Philip, even after I have been among you such a long time? Anyone who has seen me has seen the Father. How can you say, 'Show us the Father'? Don't you believe that I am in the Father, and that the Father is in me? The words I say to you I do not speak on my own authority. Rather, it is the Father, living in me, who is doing his work." (John 14:9-10 NIV)

If only we could say more often that he who has seen us has seen Jesus. And not simply as a shining example to look up to but down here, ground level, walking with others in a way where they're seen, known, and loved.

The influence of some father-son and father-daughter relationships can distort or complicate our assumptions of how God operates. While others result in a degree of hurt that I can scarcely even fathom. To this day some still carry too much anger and pain to know where to start a conversation with God the Father, assuming a part of them even wants to after all they've gone through. Hearing their stories, it's hard to blame them.

On this, though, our truer Father has profound compassion. He gave us a truer brother, and a place to begin. Not just in fact, but in sense of presence. Jesus stands there with us as we approach the mercy seat. Covering us. Sharing his own identity. Advocating. Understanding.

Interceding. Listening. Not just facing the Father but facing you and me. Reflecting the Father's face until one day the sense of dissonance recedes.

There's a very real element of waiting, a type of separation from Jesus our brother, that is a distinct aspect of our longing when it comes to him. We do have to wait a while longer before we're face to face in a literal sense. Jesus himself talked about that. He waits with us. But, in the meantime, he also asked us to be his hands and feet.

Just as relationships with our earthly fathers can make difficult our attempts to see God the Father clearly, when we think of Jesus, is he the brother who's here, the one we never had, or the one who went missing?

Give me eyes to see you, Lord. Scrub the filter I see through.

•

What caught my attention one day was this:

> May our Lord Jesus Christ himself and God our Father, who loved us and by his grace gave us eternal encouragement and good hope, encourage your hearts and strengthen you in every good deed and word. (2 Thess. 2:16-17 NIV)

Right there in plain sight. I stopped and read it twice.

It was about seeing both God the Father and Jesus being described as the comforters here. Isn't that the Holy Spirit's role? This image of both God the Father and Jesus being the strength givers and the encouragement bearers and the lovers of our souls, of my soul, was uniting to me. It gathered something back together within me. This reminder of God's unity.

It wasn't anything hidden. Sometimes we just need to rub our eyes to see more clearly.

Salvation is not a tag-team event. Though yes in physical form Jesus had to go away for a bit, he did not hand us off to the Father and the Holy Spirit. The Holy Spirit is the one who facilitates this ongoing, abiding connection to God's fullness. Jesus didn't just leave us with a part of himself. He gave us himself, period. Everything God is—Father, Son, and

Holy Spirit—speaks, listens, helps, pleads, answers, holds. Fully present. Distinct, separate, and yet very much one. And closer than this pen, this chair, and this desk I'm leaning on. Jesus sits at the right hand of the Father, but our Father is right here. No distance.

There's a mystery to the Trinity that I'll never fully grasp. The paradoxes of separateness and oneness, and of presence and waiting. But this is a season of giving myself over to mystery. Somehow all the lights are on now, and I'm in the same room with the fullness of the One I love. How is it that it's taken so long to begin to see him again?

•

Inside me, it was like there was always a packed suitcase set by the door. My go-bag for the inevitable need to move on. To keep looking. But what had I been looking for? It wasn't just about who I saw looking back at me in the mirror, it was about what I saw reflected in the eyes around me. Was I seen? Would I ever be truly known? And who would it even be safe to be known by? Who wouldn't weaponize my differences, my lack, my failures, my mistakes, allowing them to define me forever? Would there be a place I'd ever just not feel like such a stranger?

Jesus' eyes were the ones I needed to meet first. Once I was able to see how loved I remained despite all he saw, my eyes were less shaken by the eyes of others.

Right around the time I made that choice to stay put for a while, I had another dream. (Yes, I've had some doozies.) In it, dozing in the back of a car, my head on the shoulder of someone whose face I couldn't see, we rode up a mountain, eventually arriving at a cabin. So inviting but, stepping inside, it was one huge, empty room built like an awning. One or two solid walls, and the others just beams and air.

I walked to the far edge of the wooden floor, littered there with some pine needles that had blown in, vaguely aware of the others behind me unpacking the car. Pulling my sweater more snugly around me, I found that where the floor stopped so did this mountain perch. The expansive peak-after-peak view revealed us as being so much higher than I'd realized. In a heady daze, I wondered about this strange place and what this was all about.

Then, with only the slightest anticipatory tremor, the mountain violently shook and crumbled beneath me. I went skidding down the steep incline on a wave of rubble.

All came to a silent stop as distinct and final as its start. Unhurt, I crawled back up to see what was left, and nothing was. The ground had broken away starting just above where my new home had been. I remember thinking that everything I knew was gone.

Then I rose to look for people. For someone. At first, I thought I needed to find those who'd shared the cabin with me. But, no, I corrected myself, I had to find my brother. Then I corrected myself again, drilling down to the right words—not my brother by blood, but my brother in a broader sense. Then I saw I wasn't alone in my dilemma. There were now people everywhere trekking across the mountainous landscape doing just as I was. Looking for their brother. Everybody was looking, but we weren't looking for each other.

Years later now, it's a little clearer. So much rides on our individual stories. Our purpose. Our voice. Our plans. Our dreams. Our place. Our home. Our immediate family. Our inner circle. But to find my destination also meant, to a still imperfect but greater degree, finding "us."

There are ways, less than day-of-the-Lord literal but just as real and true, that I see Jesus' face from time to time. And there are few ways quite as tangible as seeing him look at me through someone else's eyes, speak to me through their voice, or work in me through their life.

> Just as the body, though one, has many parts, but all its many parts form one body, so it is with Christ. For we were all baptized by one Spirit so as to form one body—whether Jews or Gentiles, slave or free—and we were all given the one Spirit to drink. Even so the body is not made up of one part but of many...Now you are the body of Christ, and each one of you is a part of it." (1 Cor. 12:12-14,27 NIV)

An earthquake is not a private thing. As God has led, formed, grown, healed, taught, corrected, and blessed, it hasn't happened in a vacuum. In most cases we don't stay, leave, speak, listen, fight, mend, lose, win, search, find, hurt, heal, or change without other players involved or impacted. Peripherally or centrally.

God doesn't just form us as individuals, he forms us communally. One body, with Jesus our head.

•

Jesus, show us your face among each other. Help us reveal you to and see you in our sisters and brothers and, as one, show a clearer picture to those who are looking for you, too. Do what it takes in me, in us, to conform us to your image.

You do come to us even in the most solitary places. But it's moving in and with and to you that brings you to us in greater measure in each other.

•

Isa. 9:6, Matt. 12:48-50, Matt. 28:19, Luke 3:21-22, John 14:16-17, 2 Cor. 13:14, 1 John 4:11-12, 1 John 4:20-21

UNERASED

my silence
it's a part of your story
isn't it
like yours is part of mine

our stories aren't complete
without those lines listing
who's not there anymore
and who never was

silence and absence still ring in our
spirits like a bell
missing things actively present
at our tables

it's not to say we never
have our reasons
and it's not to say
they're bad ones or good
or just what we have to do

it's just to say our lives
go beyond our intentions
beyond our genres
beyond our narratives
so curated, so precious

beyond the stories we hang
on our walls in frames

we paint our stories as if the
view ends at the edges of the canvas
and compose as if we control the
dimensions of the pages we
write on, in safe isolation

perimeters clean and crisp
wide and neat
a moat with one defensible bridge
with we, the keepers of our castles, so
careful with who we allow in

our hands, our motion, our ink
but erasers don't work for us

we go unerased, no matter how we
tear the surface of shared pages
hands oscillating across them
back and forth in a blur
only to find each other still there

no, unerased and unneat
we remain part of each other's stories

we're left with
ink faded and fresh and
lines drawn through and
doodles in margins like
question marks
and darts
and flowers
and hearts

and lines drawn, left blank
underscoring silence
leaving a space
for you

MOTION

the difference between
visible and hidden
public and intimate
wind and soil
leaves and roots
heights and depths
fruit and seeds
blurs
when in motion

even embryos in stillness, waiting
are moving, becoming
racing at a pace breathtaking

roots don't just anchor
they search, travel, explore
bringing back riches from afar

A SPRING PRAYER

give me a patch of earth
to stretch within
to press against
to burrow through

give me an idea to ponder
an answer to dig for
a mystery to enter
a question to live into

give me light
to point me to the air
and rain to soften
the way

give me time
without rushing
and give me tomorrow
today

CHERYL VELK

chapter four

HONESTY + THE ALTAR

BE MY PEACE

I'm holding this so tightly
It's my security
But today's for letting go
of what's starting to own me
No one really knows but it's
time I set this at your feet
Jesus, be my Savior
Father, be my peace

Heal the thing that needs this
Shine your light in me
This one thing more I give you
I'm not afraid to let you see
No one really knows but it's
time I set this at your feet
Jesus, be my Savior
Father, be my peace

A PLACE IN ME

Lord, I've been debating your answers
but crying speak to me again
and asking why have you abandoned me
when you've just said here I am
Wringing my hands while I wring out this
fleece dripping with grace
Oh, Gideon's got a place in me
but even he found the strength
Oh, Gideon

I've been holding on to abundance
as if it were all poverty
and rambling on 'bout what I need
still hungry after the feast
Fist caught in a bottle of shiny things
holding on to me
Oh, this world has got a place in me
but it doesn't have to be
Oh, world

Don't quite know
how to give you everything
Not feeling quite strong
enough to let go
But I can do all things in your strength
and will lay all this at your feet
Lord, here is all of me
Help me hear, help me see
Help me let go
This place in me is yours alone

Lord, I've been wrestling 'til daybreak while
you just keep asking me my name
And walking to Emmaus, how could I

not recognize your face
Thought I had eyes to see and ears to hear
but I sure missed this piece, oh
Too much of me has a place in me
and it's time to be released
Oh, Savior

What would it mean
to give you everything
How would it feel
to fully let go
Oh, I can do all things in your strength
as I lay myself at your feet
Lord, here is all of me
Help me hear, help me see
Help me let go
This place in me is yours alone

LEAVES + LIVE SKIN

These ragged leaves had my attention all winter. All these leaves, more than most years it's seemed, holding on for far too long. Dead things pretending they're still alive. Or maybe it's been the trees pretending, not wanting to let go.

Who could blame them, really. So much fell last fall. Things that had been part of them.

But this spring week I keep staring at these branches budding with all this new life while still holding onto deadness and can't help thinking they're a lot like us. And thinking, "It's time."

What didn't fall last fall? What needs to? Within us, around us. From our grip. So we can more fully embrace a fresh season's beauty. Seeing the contrast—signs of new life all around—calls the question.

•

My trunk was full. Completely packed, nothing else would have fit in there. This was the first donation drop-off that downright stung. There was such a back-and-forth in me, even while walking the huge bags to the door, but I was no longer listening to the rethinking and second-guessing.

Oh, how I cringed and winced. All that excess. All that deadness. Should I have tried harder with consignment? What if I'd... But, no, I just needed to get this stuff out of my life.

I was raw, like I'd finally hit live skin. Like when you're working at a callus, filing dead skin, then there's that pink, tender layer that's getting air all of a sudden. Ouch, but something in you still says "finally."

This was bigger than Things. This went deeper than skin. This was a sacrifice and an expression of a desire for more of things that could only come from God's own hands. This was like setting my deadness on the altar. A sacrifice of what I'd held in too tight of a fist because I hadn't wanted to feel this.

With work-gloved hands, this priest in jeans took my bags.

•

Throughout all these years as God has freed me layer by layer, identifying excess and deadness around me has almost become a game. A metaphor for physically meditating upon bigger events going on within me.

Another full carload of donations went away today. And for a second time I've hit live skin. Sanding the calluses off of my life, with this layer it once again hit that point where deadness and life are so knit together, bonded past the possibility of separating them. Holding on or letting go, life is sacrificed either way. Dealing with this remaining deadness will take time and tender care.

There's a cost involved in this inner commitment to seeing deadness go. I can choose not to feel this. Many do. But I choose the brief sting of exposed rawness and life rather than the dull ache of deadness.

More so than even the first time, live skin is my heart's state in general right now. This place that's been so hard to describe even to myself and has, for probably the first time in my life, left me with no idea how to answer the simple question "how are you," it's about live skin. I've been raw and at times intensely sad, and yet things feel so joyful, positive, hopeful. Feeling a pang of joy and a pang of sorrow simultaneously—live skin is being hit in my spirit.

A callus is rough tissue that forms over a wound that gets thicker with every brush against it. But God sees through it, and through me. Ever since Eden, seems I've been covering. Now uncovered again in God's presence, letting him closer to the heart of my vulnerabilities, he's my covering. I don't need all this deadness protecting me anymore.

It's not to say all this deadness is gone yet. I keep finding dry leaves to bag up. But I've never been more sure that I'm safe in a vulnerable, unguarded state in God's hands.

•

Father God, all of this I gladly give you because I want you more. But I'm disoriented without this. What used to be a familiar picture is now a puzzle, shaken. What I reach for out of habit is gone, and it's this reminder a dozen times a day of a longing misdirected.

Defrag me, Lord. Play spiritual Tetris on me. What I've just given you has left such holes and broken connecting threads. I am a filing cabinet whose contents are scattered. I am in fragments. Put me in order. Retrain my reach and my sight. Help me see what these pieces together were intended to look like.

•

Ps. 135:15-18, John 15:1-8

YOURS

it's no wonder our churches
have that air of malls
and theaters
and coffee shops
we pick and choose what we
want of you
and when, and how

we want something other
than what laying all that down
would do to us
just you and we, with
us stripped of our vanities and
our lesser securities and
our empty hands reaching
for you
our idols set free, littering
the ground like ice from eaves

in you we live and move and
have our being, but we draw
boxes and rings and gates and
bring you bits of ourselves
like we're not all yours
and yet you stand at the door
and knock
you allow us our walls, our
boxes and gates
you want to be invited in

we're not the only ones
who lost what Eden
was about—
our own flaming sentries

try to block your way
to the deepest parts
of us

can't we give you your house
like it's yours, like it's
about heaven come down
not earth tricked out
we sing hallelujah
while holding our
other prizes tighter

I come, Lord
to your house
with my empty hands
with my agenda set down
like knees
like pages in the breeze
and sing

OFFERING

I hold so much back
I know I do
still, my meager offering
feels like everything
in my weaker moments and
by grace you move
in corners big as ballrooms
and provoke the rest of me—
the part held back—
to jealousy
for the tenderness received

WHEN WALLS FALL

A moment ago, there was darkness
Even now I can't see too far ahead
but I close my eyes and
my soul sighs as it reaches for you

And you are here in this messy place
telling me that in this moment
everything is new
just because my heart turned to you

So again, as for the first time, with
relief and joy I let another
part of me die that
kept me from you and I feel so alive

And I will enter your joy
and claim it for your glory
Count me with your cloud of witnesses
because I cannot keep this in

Here I lay it down, Lord
the thing that I've been treasuring
'cause, Lord, I want you more
Lord, I want you more

And we will enter your joy
and claim it for your glory
Tell of this day in your book of remembering
when we shouted with joy your name

Jesus... you set this prisoner free
Jesus... you loosed the chains that held me
By the power of your blood
Prompted by love for us

So here I lay it down, Lord
the thing that I've been treasuring
'cause, Lord, I want you more
Lord, I want you more

•

Josh. 6:16

MERCY

This is about more than those days I feel like apologizing for living, and for being me, and for all the things I kick myself for when I'm down. This is about more than my catalogued flaws, and falling short of who I could be, and all the mistakes that leave me wanting to start over.

Father God, there's a mark I can't hit. There's a gap your Son had to bridge for us. For me. The perfection we're told to aim for but is impossible to master. But that perfection is something quite different than self-actualization, the right sum on a quiz, or a flawlessly carried out task. Something more than avoiding a faux pas or achieving status. There are choices we make that fit a word we don't like to use—sin.

It's out of vogue, even among your own. We pray to you and commiserate with each other about our "fear of man," not hearing you ask, "You mean your pride? You mean your false gods?" Our self-will and rebellion go by so many flattering aliases, too—what must you think when we ask for your help and blessing in living them out?

There's something so unburdening about repentance. About honesty and turning toward you. Because what's waiting for us every time isn't scorn, it's your deepest love. We come away with more life, not less.

So, Father, here I am. Approaching your throne and your arms, all in one. Wanting to be in unity with you more than anything else.

There's so much I want to set down before you and confess. Those times I've refused to extend love, grace, and the benefit of the doubt. All those words I've let fly without checking with you first. Those times I've withheld forgiveness, forgetting all you've had to forgive in me. Those times I've avoided understanding another, preferring to think myself higher.

I confess I'm in need of grace, growth, and correction because we all fall short of your standard and likeness, though through our trying alone not one of us is closer to heaven.

I confess how often I've tried to do life on my own, and my delays in seeking your strength, help, and wisdom. I confess my need to hear your voice more clearly and consistently above all the other voices in the world and above my own monologuing. I confess how often I resist that, too.

As your child under grace, this confession, this repentance, isn't about legalism. It's about honoring your holiness and wanting to be more like you. And it's about desiring true freedom. Help my spirit keep straight that this isn't about earning.

•

Lord Jesus Christ, Son of God, have mercy on me, a sinner. Use even my lowest lows to glorify yourself as you daily teach and restore me. Anoint even these messes as you train me to see.

Lift this weight from me. Show me the freedom of your grace and mercy. Help me to know your compassion with what, to me, is most perplexing—when I do the things I hate and can't seem to manifest what I most want to do and be and say.

Cause me to walk in lightness and to rest in the joy of your forgiveness, help, and acceptance. You've already paid the price for this, out of love.

I want to be the one who gets it right. But what a shaky sort of security. Even when I deem myself at my best, my mixed motives, my blinders, my layers and complexities, they can still hide me from myself.

What a child's drawing even my true best can seem. And what a humbling thing when you move so visibly even within my deepest failure, weakness, and sin. Pure love, pure gift, pure sovereignty. Your grace, truth, and power breaking through my biggest cracks. The beauty all yours, but your touch bringing beauty even to what I've set down before you. Leaving me shaking my head and asking how you did that.

The power and glory are all yours, and you do much with the loaves and fishes of my life that are all I have to give you. I know it's not much, but it's all I've got.

Accept this offering. My best. My worst.

•

Ps. 26:2, Gal. 6:1-10, Rom. 2:1-4, Rom. 2:15, Rom. 7:15-23

LOVE FLOWS

Lord, did you ever run
like the prodigal's father
straight for me
Did my face cross your mind
in Gethsemane
Were you watching for me on the horizon
Were you right there in the depths of my sin
saying come home again
tears in your eyes

I can't grasp the love that flows
I can't grasp the love that flows in your veins

Jesus wept over a city
that wouldn't know him
To think that God would weep
over children who won't come home

Father, how many times
a day do you whisper
my name
Hoping that I'll stop and
listen and shift my gaze
Did you really knit me together
Could Love himself have breathed life into me
and on these dry bones
You're a mystery

I can't grasp the love that flows
I can't grasp the love that flows in your veins

Were it not for your Son
I'd think these thoughts were fantasy
If not for the price you paid
I might believe the Pharisees

At the sound of your voice
like many waters, calling me—
dry bones, they won't just stand, they'll
dance like they've never danced before

•

Luke 15:11-32

GRACE REVELATION

As I am, blood shed for me
Not what they wear, they stare
Not their size, their lives, their highs
but God's beloved, chosen

We were made free for freedom
truly free to breathe, at ease
Not false, spoken grace over
internal derision

But real lives lived are hidden
Souls hide, eyes shy, dreams fly
Hypocrisy, vanity
all just self-protection

Why? Lies, accusing eyes, or cries
like you fell, you rebelled
God whispers his grace, his face
We hear condemnation

But there's right, wrong, then the question
of regression or defection
Discern, mentor, empathize
show God's love in motion

Begun by grace, we make it
flesh's place to cultivate
Speaking liberate, we still negate
God's justification

Imperfection following
a perfect example
Bound to stumble, to crumble
lest we know restoration

As I am, blood shed for me
No plea, just me, just free
Roots deep, aim high, spirit strong
in grace revelation

•

Gal. 3, Gal. 5:1

chapter five

QUIET ME

CHERYL VELK

MAKE ROOM

Make room for new words in my heart
Empty me of all the noise
Still this spinning in me

Father, teach my soul to be quiet before thee
You know my heart's desires
I want to know yours

SKIPPING STONES

I can work a thought over
like a stone polished forever
'til it's so beautiful and shiny
how could you ever let it go

But today I'm skipping stones
and lightening my load…
I'm skipping stones

FACETS

I am a morning person, but not a Disney princess kind of a morning person. Big difference.

And I am a morning person but also a night person. This is a problem.

Basically, give me the quiet hours when the rest of the world is asleep so I can be alone with my thoughts and with God. The daytime leaves me with a lot of digesting to do. My heart and mind need time to go into that weird cabin inside myself and do that thing that would freak others out if they could only see it—staring at the pictures and notes and clippings all over its walls, with colored string on thumbtacks connecting pieces until the sun comes up.

But sometimes within I go outside, too. Where the notes are set aside, and I just want to spend time with God, and be, and listen. Finding the silence within the silence. Allowing the sediment in me to settle, bringing clarity. Revealing words that, unprompted, finally get to the crux of things.

I don't want an insular faith that only tends to myself. I want to join with others and know that sense of common pilgrimage as we walk side-by-side, tending to each other. But stepping back to this quiet place, I still myself like the earth with its seeds and receive God's light and rain. Soaking, waiting, resting, reaching. And then I enter back into the world newer, with more to give and less to circumvent.

So here I am in this quiet place, recalibrating. Allowing my eyes and ears to adjust to this different frequency. There's more going on here than it seemed in the midst of all my doing.

And here I am like the cherubim around the throne, winding down my need to speak with just one word over and over: holy, holy, holy. And gradually I get a sense of why they would find that the only word necessary.

My own words start to chatter again like water against root-exposed banks and—holy, holy, holy—God stills me.

•

Father God, you've heard me talk for hours. You've traveled with me along all the loops my mind runs in. It's a process of quieting, this winding down. Maybe, in part, you gave me a body with limits to teach the rest of me something about pacing and letting go.

If only these blocks of time could always be counted on. Sometimes the rushing river of the world doesn't let up, and it's hard to even hear myself, much less you, above the noise of the current and passing squalls. If I stop paddling even for a minute, I've got good reasons to fear what that might look like. Is it any wonder why I don't stop like this more often?

But sometimes you say "be still" not to the storm or other forces but to me. And not just in the late or wee hours but at midday. There my eyes turn to you—somehow both familiar and new—and it's no longer my world shaping me but your hands. My circumstances—these often ugly, hard things—become your artist's tools rather than instruments of destruction. Calm my vain attempts to grab them from you. Quiet me. Let me taste your strength and peace, Father. My own have worn thin.

So braced against the world's onslaught, help me soften in your presence. Form me. Shape me. This stone that I am.

•

It's become somewhat of a hobby, being a human Rorschach test. No one's immune, though the quieter ones like myself tend to leave more blanks to fill in. Once you develop a sense of humor about it, it can be kind of amusing. I don't mean to let them dig their holes deeper as they keep talking, but my mind's busy processing what their conclusions about me reveal about them in that moment.

Just as one for-instance, by different people in the same week, based on what I thought were the same data points, I was pegged as both an innocent and a party girl. Both filling in the blanks with who they'd be if they were me, neither ever actually seeing.

While others define me, like they do everyone else, through some random bias or assumption. All based on some particular detail that caught their attention. Versions of this happen all the time.

But just as common is when a friend or acquaintance sees so well a certain side of me but can lose the sense of complexity and paradox when we're in the habit of relating in a certain way. They're not necessarily wrong, though. They just have a better view than most from one particular direction or another.

I'm learning to try to help people out a little bit when it comes to all this because it's not like I don't hold wrong or incomplete assumptions about others myself. And even in the best of relationships, it's natural, fun, and healthy to still be able to surprise each other. Most of us really would like to know each other more fully. The trick is getting past the assumption that we already do. The trick is going deeper.

But there will always be those who can't or won't hear it for one reason or other. Something else is driving those concrete opinions, all mixed up and permanently set. No matter how unfair or inaccurate.

•

Father God, I used to care about all of this so much. I still do, to a point, though it doesn't rock me like it used to. Because in this quiet place you gradually got through to me, and I started being able to see myself through your eyes. And bit by bit my identity and security in you became more solid and free-standing. You stilled my failing attempts to hit moving target after moving target of expectations. You became my firm place to stand.

How can I fault others for misunderstanding or not fully seeing me when I've missed others more than a few times myself? Truth is, maybe they caught a glimpse of something that really did look familiar and built upon that. They saw something and gave it the closest name they could to try to describe it to themselves.

Here in the quiet, Lord, you haven't just shown me who I am. You've shown me yourself. But do you feel like this, too? Even with me who wants so much to really see you?

Maybe it's okay that tenderness is the facet I see in you over and over. Not in a saccharine, oversimplified, one-note way but in full strength and in all its rich complexities. It's the thing that's shone through all the different ways you've met me. A tenderness that involves both rescue and tough love walking me through growth. A tenderness that says both yes and no. A tenderness where compassion moves you to fight on my behalf. A tenderness that thought up thunder and lightning and pinecones that can only release their seeds through fire. A tenderness that's patient and persistent, never tiring. And, yes, a tenderness that says rest and eat and we'll talk in the morning. That, too.

Maybe it's okay that it's the thing I keep trying to put into words about you. Maybe it's enough for one person to try to put one of your qualities into words. Maybe that's why it takes all of us to try to describe and show the shape of you. Telling our stories and how you've met us in them.

And maybe it's why you can look so different depending on who's describing you at the moment. But you're still you and some descriptions by your friends come closer than others to the truth, while others miss you altogether.

We have the Bible as our common reference point. You gave us your Son, the Living Word, to look to and imitate. You gave your one Spirit to indwell us. It's not like we get to define you in ways that individually suit us. I'm just saying that you're the God of Thomas and the God of Simeon. The God of Mary and the God of Sarah. The God of Samson and the God of Gideon. The God of Solomon and the God of Job. The God of Leah and the God of Rachel. The God of John the Baptist and the God of the woman at the well.

Not all of them would choose "tender" among their top three words to describe you, but I bet a few of them would. And there's so much more to learn about you from the rest of them. It's we who are different, not you. Our natures, our circumstances, our stories. You reveal your one-and-the-same self to each of us in such personal ways. Different facets of your heart shining in the different lighting and shadows of different nights and days.

When I was a kid, there was this visiting preacher who slammed his fist down on the pulpit with a shout, breaking it right in the middle of his sermon. Trying to get through to us the stakes we face with you. It was the most dramatic thing to happen there in years in that more formal tradition, and we kids peered around the adults next to us, meeting each other's eyes with a mouthed "woah," trying not to giggle.

And when I was grown, there were times preachers talked about your love and grace as nothing we could earn and something lavishly and freely given while inside I was cut to the quick by your Holy Spirit about something specific I knew it was time to let go of and set before you.

You're big enough, somehow, to be in all of that and still not contradict yourself.

Even just one of your qualities, even just one facet of your nature, is endless in its richness. I could spend the rest of my life trying to put your tenderness into words and still not do it justice. Still not get to the end of it. Still not get to the end of you.

Lord, to know you at all is the tenderest, most priceless gift. Continue to reveal yourself to me. Through your Word, through your Holy Spirit, through your presence, through others sent my way in your name. I want to see whatever I'm missing that you long to reveal to me. Open my eyes, Lord, I want to see you.

And Father, in these quiet, wee hours and in these stormy mid-days— form me, shape me. Reveal your heart and your will, moment by moment, day by day. You, the great artist, working through presence and time and elements and soul surgery—all your ways are tender mercy.

Grace and mercy. For all my participation, how much has really been my doing? Other than my response to you. Other than my "yes." Other than my "please." You helping me even with that—even that is not all me. Such a mystery.

You're the only one who can picture what I and all of us together— the body of Christ—might look like after more time in your hands. The artist that you are, the vision is yours. What we become, I pray you shine through us. Reflecting your many facets in a congruous whole.

The light in this place is changing even now. You, unchanging you, are new to me every hour.

•

Deut. 32:10-11, Luke 1:76-79, 1 John 4:1-3

WORDLESS

some prayers don't
take the form of words
sometimes silence speaks best
those groanings too deep for
nouns and verbs and the
limits of our adjectives

a moment, or an hour, of
thanks, of
praise, of
gratitude, of
understanding, of
love, of
questions, of
answers, of
hope, of
trust, of
my soul immersed in yours

crying out these wordless prayers
my soul singing your name
over and over
Jesus...
Father...
Holy Spirit...
your face the wordless answer
that I run to
that I wait for

•

Rom. 8:26

STILLNESS

every leaf is still
though I thought I caught a limb breathing
where did the woman go
the one who walked down the street
like her shoulders were attached
to puppet strings
her shoulders rising, one then the other
like a seesaw
the sway swinging her legs forward
determined to make time
she walked like a clock ticking

the walkers tonight, though, are slow and drifting
their footsteps quiet
the air has stilled even the children
no shouting, no talking
one boy rides his bike in a silent figure eight
but then stops to just listen
and feel this air
the sky's deeper hue says rain is on the way
but I don't think this stillness is about what's coming
tonight there's no traveling in us
we're right here, right now
and it's enough

POISED

pen poised to write
heart reaching with all its might

like a leaf willing itself to grow
or wind telling itself to blow

it cannot force a clarity
that time and grace wait to show

staring at this page I wonder
what percolates under

and I dream about corners
and steps built for climbing
and valleys awaiting streams

holding my pen above nothing
waiting for... something

TWO SQUARE INCHES

Here's the mystery I'm left with after so many years of leaning on words: How is it that a time of wordlessness helped me begin to find my voice? It's not like I haven't spent these years pouring out my heart. In putting words away for a time, how did something clearer start to come through?

This has been a season of not knowing how to even answer someone's "how are you," this season that started when vulnerability circuits shorted out after a whole year of new writing territory and sharing. Was I running? That I didn't want to do. This quiet felt wrong and so unlike me, but necessary.

Father, you're so tender. You stilled this urgent place in me that wants to know, to rush ahead, to grasp rather than enter your rest.

Funny, your timing. After a day of mutual inspiration, I found myself swept up in a collaborative art project. One rooted in a ritual of rest and play. Just like that it was decided, and we started. Every day, more or less, for the next year, a friend and I—and another friend for a time—each drank a cup of hot tea then emptied the tea bag of its leaves. Once the day's tea bag dried, it became our canvas. We worked separately, our work our own, but there was camaraderie and encouragement in the sharing.

I didn't have to fill a whole page. I could fill two square inches with pencil and ink.

Father, in your perfect timing it was you who offered me a gentler way to speak and listen and be.

•

Sometimes wordlessness needs to be embraced rather than fought, and that's kind of where I'm at lately. Wanting to write, but not write volumes. Wanting to talk, but more so to digest and watch and listen. Wanting to form words but wanting even more to be formed.

This is rich time, not empty space. I'm quietly witnessing God at work in me and in this time. Accomplishing things that will take hindsight to fully appreciate, but he gives me glimpses. I'm wishing even now that I could say it more clearly but am resisting the urge to strip all the mystery out of mystery.

And have I mentioned yet the sweetness of spending this daily time together? At this kitchen table among tea bags and pens and pencils set out like petals and twigs, I sit with the Father, Son, and Holy Spirit in this makeshift garden, naming things.

This is a time for pressing through, but verbosity is suddenly the wrong tool. The things God is speaking, they're simple. My responses can be simple as well. The conversation is still taking place.

Some days one sentence or one word is enough and is more fruitful to the spirit than pages of revelation. Words like "I love you," "thank you," and "faithful."

Sometimes with writing it does take a few pages to arrive at those two inches. The volume that can then be condensed. Like butter, reduced over a low flame and clarified as it simmers.

But in the end it's not information I'm seeking. Or even becoming, growing, achieving. It's the Father. Even so, I'm changed in his presence.

•

Father God, you know how hard it is for me to stand down, even in solitude. The demands of action, productivity, usefulness as payment for my cosmic rent find their way even here. Some days I'm a Martha version of a Mary, if that makes any sense. My mind going a mile a minute even in stillness like a hummingbird hovering for a sip of living water. Now and then, though, I land. And rest.

Quietness can be harder than it sounds. I both loved and hated today. Asking questions I don't have the answers to yet. The determined stumbling toward epiphany, and the mystery of it finding me at the unexpected, undemanded moment. Facing what's in me and surrendering it. Listening as hard as I can to what you're trying to get me to understand, and finding you showing me rather than telling. So much gets sorted and noticed here.

It's not just you I have to humble myself before. The world has its opinions. I still feel the glares I'd get growing up if I was at rest instead of visibly active, contributing, accomplishing, producing.

And with rolled, mocking eyes, those like myself are still labeled selfish—I've heard it said from the pulpit more than once to appreciative laughter—if we take time to rest without a family to raise when there's the whole wide world to fix and save.

Here I am, that rest note again.

Those voices sound like mine now and then; I've taken over their job in my head. Judging my own introspective ways and all the recharging I need. Recharging from what, I know they wonder. If they could live in my heart for an hour, they'd get it.

It's like quiet is something we need to earn. A need we need to justify. It's like we can't just value it without commentary or defense. We risk being seen as not pulling our weight if there's any give in our weeks. White space on the page makes sense to people, but not white space in life.

True, these hours can't be commoditized. But isn't that the same perspective that's kicking art out of schools? Are we to kick it out of our churches, too? Your artistry crowded out, Lord, leaving just your metrics?

Not that there isn't art in all of it. You thought up trees that shelter and feed and are used to build useful things. But millions of them have gone lifetimes without anyone's eyes on them but yours. No one's seen their lightning strike, nutrient releasing fires or their growing. Wasted beauty. Wasted on you. By you. For you. With you.

Waste. The way that word still glares at me sometimes makes my stomach clench.

But I once got to stand in front of Michelangelo's David. As I stared up at the sculpture, captivated, it didn't cross my mind to ask what had become of all that marble chipped away. And I didn't count or judge the hours he must have spent on it. My thoughts weren't of waste.

I'm no David, but my soul feels your tools and hands forming me and taking away things in these wasted hours that I don't need. Things that get in the way of my looking more like you.

Still, I want to do more. And not necessarily even in keeping with my comfort zone, natural giftings, or perceived limits. Gideon, Moses, and a whole lot of others tried to play that card, and we all, like they, want to wave our gifting quiz results in your face. But sometimes what you ask us to do calls upon our greatest weaknesses, all so you can show your power past our limits. It's one of those ways we all need to see you. In our own lives. In each other's. In these things that, but for you, could never happen.

But I can't be everything to everyone or even live up to my own expectations. So, what do I do? I hate seeing so few bearing so much weight for the rest of us. I'm grateful for them. It's just hard to know where to start—or stop—when fresh needs keep coming to light. Sometimes I err on the side of doing too little, and sometimes on the side of too much.

Father, this world needs so much from you. As do I. And some days it's you who asks so much of me, though I won't go so far as to call that a need. And yet your wastefulness has so changed and healed me.

You didn't need to make this world this beautiful, but you did. And that beauty is both medicine and sermon. And you took six days to create what you could have done in one, making me suspect that you enjoyed the process and not just the outcome. And your Son, reflecting your nature, didn't need to spend time weeping with Mary of Bethany when her heart broke over the death of her brother, further delaying his getting on with the business of healing, but he did.

With the degree of need continually around your Son, how hard was it for him to call it a day? Was it hard for him, too—the art of leaving some things undone? How many faulted him for it? How many among that crowd pressing in? How many among his inner circle?

There are times I feel prompted to rattle off my spiritual resume. Your church still looks for titles when it comes to serving and belonging, and so when I sense that expectation I find myself pulling from a few things on the common checklist of acceptable answers—my memberships and volunteer service. Things with the word team in it, even better.

I walk away thinking of those serving in ways that cost them countless hidden hours of pondering, praying, creating, wrestling, discipling, developing, and reaching out. Meeting needs privately—anonymously, even. I walk away thinking of how many times you, through them, have changed my life.

The intercessors and prophets among us, for instance—the ones up past midnight for the sake of you and those you love so much, and willing to stand alone.

And the artists—the first ones you ever filled with your Holy Spirit to accomplish specific work, though now the church is having to relearn the value of their gifts and how to make space for their methods of communication.

The hosts—not always leading groups but initiating hours of one-on-one time with those on the fringes or setting aside their own plans and needs to minister to others. Offering presence in your name so profound that it somehow speaks all that needs saying. They give more than they receive on a regular basis.

The cycle breakers—standing in the gap between generations like Samson between two pillars, asking you for one more bit of strength to do what needs doing. Every day waging hidden battles for the sake of greater things.

And those parents who pour themselves into their children, establishing foundations of safety, love, and truth, who don't have one shred of energy left over for nursery duty on Sunday mornings. Some can't help measuring themselves against parents differently designed, supported, or challenged who do somehow make it all happen. They find it hard to see themselves shining—the God-imitating shepherds and shepherdesses leaving the ninety-nine, for a time, for the sake of the one.

All this richness, and more, plays out while the capital-d Doers rush past, some naming these servants "passengers" in the church and in ministry. Or "sideliners" when they don't sign up for the next big thing. Rushing like cars on a highway past a million flowers.

So often it's true. I know what they're getting at. So many simply attend instead of entering in. So many expect a whole lot while not wanting life together to cost them a thing. I'm only saying that it can hurt to be painted with the same brush on the heels of a week that just cost you everything.

Still me, Father. Still me. You see me. That's enough.

Help me to operate out of a place of rest. Not striving. Help me to match your pace, and to balance this doing and being in your name. Give me wisdom and peace.

Help me follow your lead in this dance. It's you I want to move with.

•

Ps. 23, Mark 6:31-33, John 11:13-37, 2 Cor. 12:9, Gal. 6:9, Jas. 2:14-17

BECAUSE IT'S LATE

the most creative thing I can do tonight is sleep
to relinquish control for a few hours
to rest, to be

the most creative thing I can do tonight is listen
to God, to my body, to snow turn to rain
and back again

the most creative thing I can do tonight is love
to wander my museum heart, portrait after portrait
then sit before one and smile or weep

the most creative thing I can do tonight is let go of this pen
to set down my burdens and let myself be loved
to let this clay soften in the warmth of God's hands

STOP

stop
just... stop
yes, you
have-to's live on either side
of this minute
but not here
not now
so stop
let grace catch up to you and
kiss you on the cheek

chapter six

THE WILDS

MOON

longest lunar eclipse of the century
and we can't see it from here
but we felt its pull
the knowledge alone enough to
increase the sense of gravity

we all leaned a little more today
on what we each lean on
who else leaned on you, Abba
is this why your Word describes you
as sitting
your lap so full of children
on days like today

STRENGTH

Chaos in the streets of my heart
burning down the gates of my mind
No reasoning today with pain
No telling it what to do

You know how my soul can get
when I'm feeling cornered
and I choose when nobody's got a
clear view of my heart but you
I'm ashamed of what I almost did
and all too often do

Is this what strength looks like—
to throw myself before you, Lord
Is this what strength feels like—
to cry out for your grace

It's taking all I've got to
search for your face again
and to trust that I'll find
your loving gaze

BLACK ICE

For seven years, home was a one-square-mile island eight hundred miles from the closest ATM, and where a light sweater was full winter gear. Then came the day we all had to leave—the project was ending, and we were giving the land back to the wildlife. So many friends today would go back there in a split second, but I'd have to think about that for a minute. For all my love of the ocean, the entire time I was there my daydreams were of mountains, forests, and seasons.

Shows and movies set in such places were a different kind of medicine after a day by the water. I'd curl up and remember turning leaves and heavy sweaters, reading books in blankets by fires, and how every few months the world would transform right in front of me. All those rich metaphors for change and everything else I was feeling. There's not an inch of creation that doesn't preach, but out of all the places I've lived, that has always been the kind of land that most speaks my language.

On Johnston Island, on any given day of the year, you could count on a blossom from the plumeria trees to put behind your ear before a night of dancing. But back on the mainland, winter is a time when the earth gets stripped bare. Evergreens stand alone, singing "life goes on" like prophets. Boundaries get blurred by snow, and sometimes fog, connecting everything, and you can't tell the gardeners from the rest of us in their season of waiting. And like the grasshopper and the ant, you discover in moments of hunger of one sort or another what's been either squandered or stored.

I learned so many good things from island friends and island days, like how to let go and just be. And how to laugh more freely. But when a couple dozen of us came to Colorado from both Johnston Island and Hawaii in those first few weeks of autumn, it was my turn to explain some things to a few who didn't yet know. Like how bridges are the first things to get treacherous when the elements turn extreme. And, whatever you do, don't get overconfident and think an SUV means invulnerability. And even when you're cautious, sometimes things will happen, so just think ahead as best you can and breathe.

•

Coming home late, wet snow had kicked in, but the highway ahead still looked clear. Illuminated crystals beyond the windshield swirled like silver starlings, and I sighed at the sweetness of being back in a place filled with this kind of magic.

But right in the middle of that thought, every tail light all at once went red. I came to a fast, solid stop a few yards behind the bumper in front of me. Nothing too dramatic, just one of those quick-reflexes-needed moments that really wake a person up. Maybe there was an accident up there—it was hard to tell. We waited a bit.

When the line began creeping, my right foot moved from the brake to the gas pedal, and I gently pressed. But there was nothing but whirring. What? My tires were spinning, and I wasn't moving. How could we have possibly stopped in the first place? The ice was so slick it took a minute of steering wheel twisting and engine revving to get even the slightest traction. I wondered if it might have had something to do with car heat, brief melting, and rapid freezing in that minute or so, except it hadn't been just under my own tires. The whole stretch from that point on had turned to glass. Including those empty stretches of road after exiting the highway.

Most days I don't notice just how protected I am—the things I've been spared by God's intervention—but that night I did. The rest of the way home I sang my thanks.

The last time I caught black ice, though, I slid. "What the..." went through my head and my whole body tensed against that sideways slide, trying to will the car in another direction. It was no use; the curb up and hit me. Hard. I know, had I relaxed into it I'd have fared better, but that was the state of my in-the-moment reacting.

Sitting there a stunned moment, adrenalin had spiked, but I wasn't exactly upset. More like relieved. Multiple sirens sounded in the distance—the whole city was going through the same thing—and they weren't for me. So much to be grateful for. My car and I were both smarting, and it would take a couple weeks and some expense for us each to stop limping, but this could have been so much worse. Thanks and praise were pouring out of me to the One whose hands I felt so safe in.

After gingerly taking a penguin-walk lap around the scene to see what the damage was, barely staying on my feet on that skating rink, I awkwardly swung back into the driver's seat, almost falling, and calmly thought about my options. That's when I caught my eyes in the rear-view mirror. I nearly laughed as I asked myself, "Who even are you, anyway?" Not that long ago so much less would have sent my spirit into a skid, careening.

•

Black ice can scare you to death. You think conditions are clear but then a patch of invisible slickness takes your feet out from under you and you don't have the traction on your world that you thought you did. You hit the ground so hard and fast that it punches the breath right out of you, and pain shoots from one to ten in an instant. Who could have ever expected that? At least right there and then. There's no way to brace yourself for it or plan your reaction. It happens way too fast. And sometimes it's no blip in a season; it kicks off a total change in life's direction.

It's taken me out too many times to count in one form or another. Does this, to some degree, miss anyone at all? It's not just about the weather. And not everything we get to walk away from. A diagnosis comes when a test was supposed to be routine. An unexpected expense or market drop hijacks your plans and sense of security. An industry shift takes your job from cutting edge to stone age. Someone your world revolves around tells you they're leaving. A child stops meeting development markers. An aging parent begins to forget things like faces and eating, and you're the one they have to lean on.

Black ice. No traction on this world's surface. In what direction do we fall?

So many things upend and bring-to-our-end us. Reframing entire identities. Disrupting our sense of security. We thought we'd built our lives on such solid ground and been so methodical with our steps. We couldn't have been more careful. We had dreams and a plan, and we chose as best as we could, but life doesn't always cooperate or make sense.

The hows and whys of all these things are more complex than any simplistic statement can lump together, at least for me. Who's to blame? Is it so simple?

Something foundational went awry way back when with mankind telling God with our actions that we want what he has but would rather have our autonomy. Not understanding that what he has just doesn't work the same without him; it relies on him. Self-sufficiency—the idol whose strength he allows us to test. Loss of unity with him—what happens to an engine when you throw in a wrench or a part goes missing? Breaking. So much breaking.

So many hard things we don't bring upon ourselves. We're in a world off-track. There are things that won't be fully set right until heaven, but our God can redeem even this. He has not left us comfortless or without hope. So often, yes, there's miraculous reprieve, but he moves in strength even within what we hate and fear most.

I wish you could sit with one of my closest friends who has an aggressive, late-stage cancer and witness how she talks of little else but God's kindness and faithfulness. Without fail, our conversation just gravitates there. Not the hyper-positivity that often marks the start of a battle this big, still detached from the potential long, hard road ahead. But the softened grace and purest joy and compassion of a life held by him. Tempered by the realities of and, yes, grief over all she and her family are facing. Her life, her journey, her changed countenance have shown me more of God's tenderness than any one miracle I've witnessed ever has.

•

Something more than love is at the core of this world's season. We're in a battle. And, more than anything else, it's a battle for our hearts.

> Be alert and of sober mind. Your enemy the devil prowls around like a roaring lion looking for someone to devour. (1 Pet. 5:8 NIV)

Yes, him. Erase from your mind the cartoon images that try to diminish what we're up against and disarm us in the process. Look around and within and consider the possibility that sometimes you're wrestling with more than just yourself, and that we fall prey to actual schemes and tactics. Consider that evil is something other than a faceless force, and that there are many players engaged in the power play of all power plays. Some we can see, and some we can't.

You can hear it a hundred times, but strange how it took some time in the wilds for me to begin experientially learning and believing that the deck is actually stacked in our favor. Especially when some harder circumstances haven't let up.

> What, then, shall we say in response to these things? If
> God is for us, who can be against us? (Rom. 8:31 NIV)

I'm not saying I never get shaken up anymore, fall for dark lies, or overthink myself into a quagmire. Even Elijah went running on the heels of his part in one of the most epic displays in history of God's power and sovereignty, so how about we give ourselves a break in the midst of our learning curve.

What I'm noticing, though, is that it happens less. And the lies get recognized so much more quickly. There's more peace and trust where my knee-jerk reaction used to be fear. Knee-jerk trust, how's that for a plot twist. And there's more security, confidence, and anticipation where there used to be master class what-iffing.

Many of the circumstances we find ourselves in are nothing short of agonizing. I won't even attempt to throw a prettier filter on those pictures. That's not what this is about.

The thing that never stops amazing me is how God's used these things in spite of themselves to grow and shape me, and how I've seen myself trusting God's goodness and faithfulness more and more implicitly. No matter the outcome of any given storyline.

It's God's artistry, compassion, and warrior strength that meets me in the wilds and reminds me to look up and remember him and, in him, who I am.

There is no formula for how God meets us within this infinite variety of circumstances and moments. But he does meet us.

A couple decades ago I wrote a bad song. But I've always liked the chorus, and it's still the thing that springs to mind, the thing I need to sing, those moments I land hard on another patch of ice. The chorus goes:

> So what's it gonna be?
> What's it gonna be tonight?
> Sometimes you show me your glory.
> Sometimes an angel gives me bread.
> Sometimes you help me find my fight.
> Sometimes you open up your hand.
> So what's it gonna be?
> What's it gonna be tonight?

I've kept the verses together with it all these years, as much as they make me cringe. Not that I've ever shown them to anyone, I just never threw them out. With others I've tossed the parts I don't like without hesitation, but I never quite did with this one. The reason was never clear enough to me to say. But today it reminds me how once in a while, even in the middle of what you hate, you can find something you'll hold on to the rest of your life.

•

Phil. 4:11-13

CHERYL VELK

WAR

it was my first East Coast snow
all the neighborhood kids were
at war, the cul-de-sac snow fort
begun by the plows, a story
high now, was the territory fought for
the storm of snowballs half ice
thrown like killing words hit deeper
than my body, I think they hit my soul
five was so far from four
east was so far from west
I just wanted to survive
I just wanted to go home

MEMORIAM

when wound becomes shrine
when pain becomes stone
an object with weight and boundary
and eerie beauty
bowed before, worshiped,
tended to like a grave

yesterday becomes
forever, forever
a shadow sighing, defining
the weight and boundary
of songs and of souls

cold, dead things
that never
move

DETOURS + DEAD ENDS

There are stains we let sit until it seems nothing can remove them. There are cuts untreated that become infections spreading. There are broken bones unset that get a person growing crooked.

There are wounds we wrap ourselves around for protection in a way that becomes a new inner posture, an inner armor. Until that poisoned arrow lodged, with nowhere else to go, becomes a dark jewel in a treasure box that we've lost our own map to.

Never mind the world's scale of acceptable pain levels and reactions—for you it was an earthquake. It tore up earth within you and reshaped the landscape. And never mind how much time has passed since then—here you are, right now, still living its aftermath.

There are roads we take, never believing we could get so lost. Turns left or right. Doors walked by or walked through.

There are words that can't be caught back and unspoken, and actions that can't be undone or forgotten. They set too much in motion.

It's hard to face, but we've borne our own quiver of sharpened arrows, too. Some made clumsily in haste, in play or the urgency of the moment. And some fine-tuned at length with museum-worthy artistry. Exquisite weapons flying. Words and plans unmistakably crafted and polished.

Conversations were rehearsed and, whether or not they've ultimately taken place, we've lived out that heart place.

Sometimes all it takes is a fleeting look in the eye. A picture worth the thousand bitter words harbored against the ones we have in mind—and the ones who remind us of them. Sometimes all it takes is that look to pierce and make bleed. Looks of anger, smugness, or dismissive assumptions. A snub. A snap judgment. Coldness. A joke said with a smile that denies the pointed intention.

And some days the one we're most cruel to is ourselves.

We walk away not always knowing which arrows killed or maimed their prey, lay unspent in that field, or were surgically removed and the injuries healed. We don't always know the impact of our presence. Even on ourselves. We don't always realize the cumulative effect of the things we tell ourselves. The arrows that find us that we twist and push deeper.

It's not just them. It's we. It's me.

By the time I dared look, my heart was a battlefield. No longer fully able to tell what damage was from friendly fire or the enemy.

•

It was a favorite hymn from earliest years, and I was five again and singing. In my mind's eye, a familiar hand long gone reached out to me. Not at all who I expected. Why was it as if my dad was there?

"God, I can't. I won't. It's okay if he just sits here, but more? What's the point? I'm just not ready. Take this arrow from my heart—the one I know is in me. Please. I'm offering it to you. Take it."

"That's not how this is going to work. Hand it to me. Take his hand."

My dad in heaven about a decade and a half by then, we were overdue for a healing conversation. Is it enough to say he'd been human, and that despite all his brilliance and other reasons for admiration he'd had his own demons to fight? And, like the rest of us, he wasn't immune from that making for some collateral damage.

It took me a few minutes to wrestle with the request. Take his hand—really?

This isn't the type of thing I can see him asking everyone. Not all forgiveness need look this way. But in this mishmash of love and hurt with this particular person, there was something God wanted to not just free me from but restore to me.

I thought I'd already forgiven. Thought I'd already moved on. I've since learned that grieving and processing happen in layers.

I slid my open hand across the empty chair next to me, pantomiming this act. Something in me still suspects I closed my hand on more than just air.

One arrow removed. The oldest. The sharpest.

I don't know how much my dad heard of what I said later that night. I only knew that by morning I was further down the river, carried by all that water under the bridge.

•

It was a men's retreat, with a chance to work behind the scenes. Blessing and ministry, en masse, by proxy. They weren't the ones who'd hurt me but enough people in the past had, and all too often with my own misguided cooperation, that I'd grown guarded and less than my truest self in their presence.

When this opportunity to serve arose, the words that came to mind were, "Wash their feet." I thought of Jesus just before he was betrayed, taking that posture. Showing what it meant to live like him. Shattering his disciples' ideas of what seemed right or appropriate.

Framed arrowheads on the mountain lodge wall struck me as a promise in the midst of this inner narrative. And by the end of the weekend, a second arrow was removed from within me.

It was more than symbolic. The whole weekend was a spiritual battle. It was a weekend of warfare in prayer for them, for me, and for the friend I was serving with. And the physical demands of meal preparation for all of the camp's guests, not just ours, were more than we'd anticipated or were up to, but we somehow got through it. I never expected it to be that hard. Or for it to be about so much more than just me. Or for the degree of release to be quite that profound.

•

It was a small, bright blue box of art supplies. Formerly a childhood toolbox of my father's, last name scratched into the lid. Drawing pencils and tools were inside that I hadn't touched since the day my creative spirit got brutalized and went into hiding. A professor who reveled in shaming all but his very few stars had left me floundering. To be honest, I hadn't been at all ready for the risks of self-expression, and so was far from equipped to deal with that kind of viciousness. At a vulnerable time when I should have come into my own, I folded. I changed majors to one that leaned more on facts; things outside of myself that I could defend with research.

"Open it up," God nudged me as I held the box. I did and, with the same metallic clunk, another drawer of my puzzle-box heart popped open. Another arrow was revealed and given up. And the voice echoing in that chamber finally stopped.

This puzzle box type of mystery to the order of my opening and freedom was something only my Designer could have figured out. Only he knew the order in which these more hidden drawers needed to open so other arrows could be released. And the location and operation of each trigger mechanism. And that it was time for this particular one.

·

Miraculous, healing power, and yet a combination of heart, action, and will had been required of me. Acts of forgiveness. The most excruciating relief.

More time went by and, one by one, more arrows were handed back over to the Master. Redirected and repurposed, added to his arsenal for the part of the battle we can't see. And with each one, more and more began changing.

The weapons themselves were gone now, but the effects had reached deeper than they'd ever hit. Now, though, there was finally a fighting chance for that to be addressed.

With surgical hands, God took me layer by layer to the most hidden pockets of infection.

There was one arrow left, though, that was beyond my reach. No act of willpower was enough when the one that needed forgiving was me.

It was after the fact that God directed my attention to the place where that particular arrow had been. Shame. How could I have offered it to him; I could only offer me. Somehow he worked it loose while I wasn't even looking, then woke me to smile and draw my attention to the freedom.

·

Father, Most High, Elohim. There's a way the most beautiful, miraculous moments in this world bring us to our knees. The world stops as we even just barely begin to understand what the word holy means. It's only the smallest taste of who you are, and it makes us want to stay there forever, singing, "Holy, holy, holy."

Things never should have been this way. My own darkest moments and those of others. Offending you and often causing injury to lives, minds, hearts, bodies, souls. Flood this darkness in and around me with your presence, your light, your mercy, your healing. Your kingdom come, your will be done. On earth. Among us. In me.

Give my heart and life this day's manna. A sip from your cup. A swim in your river. Strength to climb. Joy in your presence.

Mercy and justice, God, mercy and justice. Whether wielded by myself or others, every one of these arrows was also aimed at you. The wounds your Son bears aren't just in his side, hands, and feet.

Forgive me, God. Forgive me. You know the memories and realities rising.

Give me the strength to forgive as you've forgiven, so you can have your fuller way within me. I want this release, so I hand you everything.

And since I now need to learn a new way of moving forward, lead me. Deliver me. Smooth the ground ahead to help keep me from stumbling. You know what's most likely to get me falling. You know where evil lies in wait along the road I'm on. Please walk with me. I don't know the way, but with you even right here is life and grace.

Walk me through all this unwinding. Layer by layer, unfamiliar turn by unfamiliar turn. Get to the heart of me and breathe.

This is your land, Father. My heart, my life. Reclaim and restore it. Tend this land with me—this garden needs some work—and walk here freely. I'm yours.

•

Isa. 2:4, Isa. 35:3-10, Ps. 37:14-15, Matt. 11:4-5, John 13:14, 2 Cor. 10:3-5

AMONG LIONS

my soul is among lions
their teeth are spears and arrows
set for me

but I trust in you and all is quiet
in the shelter of your wings
there is mercy

mercy and truth, a secret shelter
within the tempter's den
among the hungry

•

Ps. 57:1-4

ACHING AFTER ANSWERS

Aching after answers
like the sighing of the wind
I'm all out of words except
Lord, hold me close again
Hope's got a melody
quiet now, I need it loud
And your love's got colors that
I just can't live without

I can't form the question
my soul's asking day and night
Lord, I'm asking anyway
read it better than I
Grace has got a language
higher than these words can know
Father, would you speak to me
there's nowhere else to go

Lord, here's my heart
Here are my fears
Lord, here's my mind
Here are my tears
Lord, here's my life
Here are my days
Lord, here's my trying
Here's my staying

Not sure what I'm asking
you to speak to in my soul
Just sure I'll see your face by
the time you let me know
You are digging deeper
than I ever thought you'd go

And I'm already reaping
far more than I have sown

Not out of the woods yet
there's a long way left to go
You know I'm lacking patience
on this unending road
Help me see the beauty
of light sifting through the leaves
While you sift through my spirit
to free the you in me

•

Rom. 8

CHERYL VELK

chapter seven

GROWING

CHERYL VELK

BLOOM

"Son, here's a dollar," he folded paper money
into the small hand of the man of the house
entrusting his rose-red ministry for
a week since this one might wilt and
he could picture her smile at the gift from
thousands of miles away, just like the first one

So a boy's brows bent in concentration, and serious
eyes searched through misty glass for perfection in
a strong bud held high because he knew
the most tightly wound ones last
though sometimes, too, the neck will droop before
full bloom... but, "that's life," Dad would say

a little angry,
but what can you do

Postcards of pyramids and dancing ponies
with notes just for me by his own hand said
Thanksgiving was lonely and when he
came back sometimes the door would slam
as saturated years weighted his joys
and birthed 2 a.m. fears of never retiring

But he wrapped wonder in big red bows as he
built a fire and showed us things we'd never known
Weeping glaciers, my first turquoise ring
a buffalo bounding across the road—
Dad, did you see how big he was... summers whispered
riding quiet comfort in a downpour

and little ears listened from landings
for shouting or whistling

Some grey set in before the box of office burdens
brought home each day grew lighter as sun and sea
coaxed him to live and, floating there in wordless
grace, he tasted the salt and was thirsty again
So he let breezes gently unfurl the life God
had gifted him with before the race ever began

"Such a handsome man," the stranger nudged my mother
with a smile and watched him stride with a wink
and a grin to greet his wife with a kiss
and dancing purple orchids to bless her neck
so she sat in his lap to laugh for the cameraman
two kids on a second honeymoon captured in time

pressed in a book
found in a frame

blue shirt
golden hair
purple orchids
white, white smiles

just in time

Because just two weeks later the same pair sat
side by side and numbly heard you have a year
no, six months... then, I'm sorry, it's the worst kind
so you'd best find your last words
Four weeks and a day, to be exact
though the last two, well...

Not much time, but time enough
for little things
and little words

His driver's license and credit cards in a neat
narrow row on the bureau, next to his penny bank
That penny bank... I'd always wondered why that

black-overalled man with the flat hat and the
slot in the back made the cut with each move…
You need to get out, Cheryl, help your brother pick out pants

You can leave the skin on the chicken tonight
Here, have a Ghirardelli chocolate from the
thinking-of-you bouquet from your sister
I'll have one, too
Green, blue and burgundy wrappers fell
like wildflowers on the table between us

We'll be okay, us three
mother, brother, and me

"How's it going, kiddo?" "I'm okay, Dad, the guy
you never liked is gone—the one you called a coward
for never looking you in the eye"
You just nodded, peaceful, and ate your ice cream
and didn't even quiz me about when I
was getting that master's and Ph.D.

"We were supposed to grow old together," she choked
then stopped herself, turning away
wouldn't show him so much pain
so she looked back with a deep breath
and a nod and tears in her smile
because there was nothing more to say

Nothing… and everything

So my brother raged and mother prayed and I wrote
pages and pages in quiet places and for
five years, ten months and some-odd days was
bound and angry but then somehow forgave
the things unmended
the things unintended

and dreamt again of buffaloes in bows
big as the great big sky
running across the road

Then I danced a starry night away
unbound, unwound

'Cause what's it all about, anyway
if you don't go ahead and bloom one day

THE BEAUTY OF IT ALL

you put me back together
and gone are some things
that never belonged

what's left is starting to look
more like you and more like
the me you meant all along

while I go round and round
I'm still on your wheel
potter shaping clay
on a day
that still looks the same to me

then comes the fire
then comes the beauty of it all

GROWTH

what is growth
is it skill, is it knowledge
is it will, is it wholeness
is it a moral compass
is it something you
participate in
or just let happen
does it come from discipline
or a simple stretch
toward the sun

a child will grow to adulthood
with no say in the matter
but sometimes you can see
the difference between childlikeness
and perpetual adolescence

honed skills or natural talent may gain
a growing stack of accomplishments
and charm and grace may
win favor and entry to circles of choice
but a widow's one cent
offered up out of love—
so unimpressive, but all she has—
gets the attention of heaven

•

Mark 12:41-44

ALIGNMENT

Some kids seem to grow without ever experiencing what anyone else would call an awkward year. Growing with the beauty and ease of an ice crystal on glass, its pattern expanding perfectly until it fills the whole window. No research paper explaining the mechanics of it will ever keep us from staring in awe at the artistry.

Others, like me, have always grown unevenly. Like trees. Losing and gaining many times over the things that make them most valued by others. Bending and sometimes one particular limb breaking with the weight of a harder season. Branches taking new directions, abruptly.

I watched a certain tree out my back window for years, wondering if it would ever bounce back from a drought that had taken most of its leaves and vitality. When it did erupt with green life like someone had pulled the ripcord on a parachute, the sight of it stole my breath. Ugly for a time, so raggedy and right in my sightline, I had started to wonder when they'd give up and just cut it down. But somebody had more faith than me and, sure enough, it didn't just make it, it flourished.

It can be hard to wait our growing out.

•

I was one of those teens who could talk to adults with ease but had a little more trouble feeling out life with those my age.

Some tried to tell me my differences were good, and a time or two I even tried to tell myself. But it was too hard to accept in the face of the loudest message that had won my attention and belief. I internalized the idea that you have to figure out what people expect of and want from you and, at all costs, give it to them. Like the right answers on a multiple-choice quiz rather than an essay answer open to opinion. There was little sense of okayness as-is when everyone around me was trying to figure out our places—theirs and mine—in life's pecking order. Different wasn't safe, and all I knew was that I didn't quite fit in.

Much of my growth, for sure, has been about learning and healing. And much of it's taken certain disciplines, as if your heart and mind are instruments and the scales take practice before better music can start flowing.

But when I think of my biggest strides forward, they've had to do with alignment of will with my Designer. Trusting his goodness and love and the richness of the story he's telling, and my place in it and in him.

•

It can be difficult sometimes not to resent or at least struggle with the hand you're dealt. Circumstances permanent to fleeting, inconsequential to all-encompassing, they can all raise similar questions and feelings.

We're challenged, pushed, traumatized, robbed, capsized, hurt, and next thing we know we're a stranger to both ourselves and others. Is it always fair to say this is who we were all along? Some events do change us, or at least beg the question of direction. There are identities we embrace and abandon in such moments and seasons.

> Dear friends, do not be surprised at the fiery ordeal that has come on you to test you, as though something strange were happening to you. But rejoice inasmuch as you participate in the sufferings of Christ, so that you may be overjoyed when his glory is revealed. (1 Pet. 4:12-13 NIV)

What feels so unfair and like an interruption of our real life is so universal and daily. This, not that clear-sailing phantom, is our baseline. Don't be surprised. Expect to be tested.

I recognize care is needed in using this passage—in using it to talk about anything other than people being tortured, harassed, or driven out of home or livelihood because of their faith. Persecution is real, and let's not compare a flat tire—or even a serious health battle, for that matter—to a church in flames.

And yet this still brings to mind what it's like not just to suffer because you're a Christian but to suffer all things as a Christian.

A few chapters earlier, Peter seemed to allow for that:

> In all this you greatly rejoice, though now for a little while you may have had to suffer grief in all kinds of trials. These have come so that the proven genuineness of your faith—of greater worth than gold, which perishes even though refined by fire—may result in praise, glory and honor when Jesus Christ is revealed. (1 Pet. 1:6-7 NIV)

How many times have I heard "suffering"—said ironically with quote fingers—mocked. But no measure of alignment of will is a small thing. In reading these verses, there's such recognition and gratitude, because it's not just persecution that can cause faith to fail. It's not just mocking or attack that can make one's heart ache like Jesus' heart did. As if we can separate doing battle with the world, powers, and principalities from the battle within ourselves.

Jesus, before his ministry began, was tempted in the desert with an appeal to his hunger, with a challenge to his identity, and with misdirected worship as a shortcut to a lesser glory. Gethsemane the night before the cross wasn't the only place his alignment with the Father was proven.

In Eden, way back at the beginning, there was a lie believed. Hadn't God, it went, actually said it this way? Does he really have your best interests at heart? Did you know you can be just like him? This looks good, doesn't it—what's stopping you from taking it?

In the desert, the same voice tried the same thing with Jesus and was defeated. In our deserts, the same voice never tires of posing these same questions.

•

Harder circumstances are nothing I face with a sense of resignation. I fight and pray, and I rejoice when victories come. It's just that someone is always going through something with no instant, easy escape. And every victory is eventually followed by another challenge.

We're drawn to stories full of struggle. We turn off the news we've been riveted to, feeling ill from it, but then turn to a movie for more of the same themes. But it's for the overcoming and rescue that most of us dive in. "Please tell us good wins," we say, turning to glowing screens. We seek release in tales that speak to our heartache, frustration, fury, and dreams. Tales that supply happy endings or we hope will help us understand.

But I've walked out of theaters shell-shocked, too; drop-kicked in the chest by stories with no such resolution. What agony to know that's what suffering and struggle are like for so many. I've felt it, too, in my darkest times of questioning.

No matter the various reasons why we face what we face, God offends our sensibilities now and then when he lets us walk through it. Wouldn't real love make this go away if it had the power to? Why does he allow it?

To hear a word like "testing" at such a time can be wrenching. But this isn't about telling a hurting person that God is trying to teach them something, like the darkest evil or pain in the world is a lesson by a cruel headmaster. No, testing, more than anything else, is about revealing. There are circumstances that aren't lessons, and yet within them we still choose and the Holy Spirit still moves. Or we block that movement and say, "maybe later," or "never." Some within suffering move further from God's heart, some move deeper into it, and some don't move at all. Complexities and mysteries abound in the who and when and why of it all.

As the truth of ourselves is exposed, God is right there to comfort and strengthen us. And yes, to develop us, too. Despite so much ugliness, something beautiful and important can happen here when we turn to him. Art emerges from the fire. We become something new.

We come to God as we are. We, the thirsty, the hungry. We, the ones who take him up on the invitation to call him Father. We who need him. We who take hold of his grace. We come as children, but what good father doesn't offer his kids wisdom or prepare them for adulthood? Those are the fathers we call the best ones.

We come to God as we are, turning away from our old way of being. Indwelled by his Holy Spirit, he becomes our new center. Our greatest desire. Our new reference point. Our new anchor. In the act of turning in this new direction, we find ourselves changed already.

Sitting right beside us in church are many of those whose mouths have said "Jesus is Lord" without that turning of heart, mind, and spirit, and the Bible warns us that they're not actually his. What's more, it says it will come as a surprise to many of them. This is about more than intellectual assent. The Bible says that the demons, too, believe—and they tremble.

Among those who come to God truly—Father, examine our hearts, keep us from self-deception—we come as we are but are not meant to stay that way. Walking with God in a living, active way means growth and change.

And, the thing is, who steps into maturity without a fight? I think of maturity here as stepping more fully into who God made us to be and his counter-cultural ways. Something that will always go against what we'd rather do, say, believe, or be at some point, or take us someplace other than where we'd prefer to run, hide, or stay.

What else could rounds of dying to self and growing pains and pruning—oh Father, the pruning—possibly feel like, except for trial?

We're going to be exposed at some point, even just to ourselves. Life has a way of doing that. But what we do with that information is what our stories hinge on. It's where the plot thickens.

Gethsemane wasn't just a dark place of lamentation and solitude on one night. It was a place Jesus went often to spend time with his Father. To talk. To ask. To listen. To rest. And he often brought his friends. And, yes, it's where he fought to keep his heart, mind, and will in alignment with the Father's and fight for that surrendered yes. Gethsemane is one of those places we go as we imitate him.

I've had some harder Gethsemane moments these past years. After this last one, I remembered some lyrics I'd written a couple decades ago. In part:

> I'd rather laugh than cry, Lord. Rather dance than fall
> to my knees. I love the sun more than freezing rain and
> abundance more than need. But I love your comfort
> and how you lift me up. And I love your shelter from
> the bad things that come.

Bones are bruised from this journey, and these rags are stained and old. And I can't run my fingers through the tangles in my soul. 'Cause like a child I want it easy, and as years go on I want it now. Yet this time is here to lead me to a better place somehow.

So will you refine me like something of value? And will you test me as a precious thing? Will you let me believe these rags hide splendor? Please let me see what you created me to be.

Preserve me through the fire, melt impurity from purity. I'll endure the pain and take the time if you'll just make me holy. If you will give me hope, Lord. Oh, if you will call me yours. Mold me and make me completely yours.

And that's what God's been doing. Somehow using everything that's come my way—the good, the bad, and the ugly—to answer that prayer. That yes. He's used that willingness to face the fires that come now and then. From within them I hear Nebuchadnezzar cry, "Do you see it? She's not alone there in the fire." And once released from them I hear him say, "Look, she's unharmed and doesn't even smell like smoke."

God has called us out of darkness into his marvelous light. And with each descent we make into a difficult yes, he lifts us back to his light. Growing us. Making us more like his Son. And as God lifts us to wave after wave of new life after each descent, each round of dying to self, we arise truer to that identity.

Be truly glad. There's wonderful joy ahead.

•

Ps. 105:19, Zech. 13:9, Matt. 7:21-23, Jas. 2:19, 1 Pet. 2:9, Heb. 12:1-2

PIECES

the past is falling away in pieces
like scales from a blind man's eyes
like snow from a boot on a welcome mat
like layers on that first warm day of spring

I felt the aching groan in my bones
in my cells, in my skin
then the great crack as the
mountainside shook off all that was
too weak in its grip
but there was no terrifying roar
it just... wasn't there anymore

with whispers of grace, grace
some dreaming part of me threw off
these covers in the dark
and wondered at the warmth of the waking light

THE RACE

Most people never get to be the best
Most people fall short of the rest
in their own eyes from time to time

What then is all this about
running the race to win
when this body is broken
like now and then my will

They're so far ahead of me
what's so special 'bout where I am

But still you died for me
and your love keeps moving me
to get back up and lift my cup
and fight for this race I'm in

As if I'm the only one running
into your arms

•

1 Cor. 9:24

BREATHING + WEAVING

A small group of us shivering in a row. Boys and girls sitting on the edge, feet dangling in the water. All of us at three or four, first experiencing the great, big pool. Older kids at the other end, laughing and squealing. We lived by the ocean, and there were things best learned early.

"Stop crying," he'd say, and hold us under until we stopped fighting.

We learned to swim, and other things, too.

That was insane, I tried to say, rushing away, shaking. But instead of expected defense and sympathy there was smiling, shrugging, and a quick squeeze. Some things in life you just have to do. You're no longer a baby.

Few others seemed to get upset. We were all the same age. What was different about me?

Over the years, lesson after lesson got caught into fibers all woven together into bigger stories. From home to church to school buses to executive offices, my head collected evidence, my heart collected memories. Finding what I expected to see, again and again.

These things settled in. These fibers getting more and more clogged with the years, and out of silence and acceptance never getting cleaned. These patterns, these woven fibers, became the rug I walked on and the filter through which I saw everything. This was just the way life was, and this was my place in it. Too many people agreed. What was the use in questioning?

In the years that followed, I'd wake up remembering dreams where I was immersed in water but could breathe. Letting go of the tiled side of the swimming pool after letting myself sink, I heard muffled talking and playing above me. I opened my eyes to see kids' shimmering colors dart past, along the side, like schools of fish on land. That's when the possibility occurred to me. And, as crazy as I knew it sounded, I had to see. Through teeth lightly clenched I parted my lips and inhaled slightly, and pure, fresh air filled my lungs and my whole being. Muscles relaxing but holding my mouth just so, I got the hang of it quickly. Excited and joyful, off I went swimming and exploring. No longer afraid of drowning, because now land and seas and swimming pools were all the same.

If only not-drowning were that easy. In waking life, I didn't pick it up quite so naturally.

•

Sometimes love is a shake. Sometimes love brings you to the end of yourself. And with compassion in its eyes, rather than the bored coldness of that suntanned teen, it brings you to the end of your control and strength and the end of your doing and reasoning.

Sometimes love is like darkness and water to a seed cracking open, dying in a way that leads to its fullest expression.

It caught me completely off guard. News that had unleashed hope and joy, my soul thinking it was safe to let out those dreams, the intensity and even existence of which was shocking to me. Who knew all that in concentrated form had been hiding in crevices that deep? Only to be followed so close on the heels by the same old story. News that said you celebrated too early, life's the same as it ever was. Fooled you, keep swimming.

Except this time, I wasn't braced for it. Heart cracked open too wide, it had hit too deep, and there was mayhem.

It was like Pandora's Box opening, except it was hope and beauty escaping that had me whirling and grieving. Put it back, please put it back. Just look where it got me.

What would either answer now tell me about God, myself, healing, prayer, confidence, faith, hope? I didn't know anymore; I just didn't know. And what was I to do with all of this I never realized was in me?

All I knew was I needed to find the place with God and life where either outcome would tell me the same thing.

Emotional and spiritual whiplash. My soul a rug God had taken by the edge with a snap and a shake. Dirt and dead things flying from where they'd been lodged and caked.

But he never said stop crying. He knew what this was taking. He stayed, I stayed. His eyes were firm but loving, and he really saw me. I hadn't yet learned but, bewildered, it dawned on me that I could breathe.

Where all this would take me, I didn't know, but for the first time I knew I was strangely safe.

•

The shake was one thing, but then came the deeper cleaning.

Three years later, the fibers in me were still being cleaned. Life just wouldn't stop, and it felt like churning and scrubbing. One after a ridiculous other the crises came. Wave after wave.

This soul weaving, this rug, this filter in me was now in the heavy-duty cycle. Getting tossed around and overwhelmed, then spinning, then the world filling and churning all over again.

But the Holy Spirit was in there with me. And I began to notice colors emerging. This was all working the deepest stains loose. This was what it was taking to release what I'd thought was part of me. As more and more was released, I started to see differently.

Despite all my requesting the delicates cycle and some steady, comforting soaking, a little spiritual Jacuzzi with a cocktail, there came the harder need to say, "Okay... (deep breath, but...) yes, God." Nothing about it easy but coming to respect and even strangely love the waves throwing me into the arms that kept catching me.

Because he kept catching and catching and catching me. He kept speaking, holding, strengthening within the churning. As each wave came, I found myself more quickly expecting God's anchoring and asking how he would show me his face.

Despite all this was requiring of me, this was nothing I was doing. God himself was strengthening my believing. Increasing joy and peace. Retraining my eyes to see. Teaching my lungs to breathe.

•

Father God, had I suspected I'd find myself here experiencing this kind of freedom, I would never have fought the process as much as I did or relied so heavily on my own reasoning. But that was part of my deal. A big part of what needed growing and freeing.

I didn't even know what I was praying for when I first cried "help," but you saw all the way to the origins of every strand in this tangled mess.

140

Like a Gordian knot, I would have taken a sword to it, but you were patient. You saw my heart, not a problem to bypass. Through my disposable culture's fast-paced eyes I judge myself, but you built me to last and considered me precious.

You've always answered ten levels deeper than I've known to ask.

This promised land, Lord. It was worth those years. Just to be with you here has been worth my whole life. And from this vantage point, it's like you've redeemed my whole story.

•

Phil. 4:13, Rom. 15:13, Jas. 1:2-4

NEW

this cold spring night, it is
cutting right through me
rain reaching my bones
like a song speaking truth
broken wide open, I
lean into earth and
pull tight these covers
and I wait to be new

does a tree feel its rings
like I feel these days
forming me slowly
through elements and grace
does a branch feel the weight
of budding new life
like my deep-bowed head
nearly touching terrain

I look to the mountains
then look to my hands
the help that I need
is beyond both of these
oh, make me be something
you meant from the start
I pray every day
as I watch for your dreams

and I sing to you
like all creation's gotta do
if I don't, stones will have to

•

Luke 19:37-40

chapter eight

HOPE + TRUST

POOR MAN'S FAITH

is hope really poor man's faith
like they always told me
'cause faith, hope, and love keep
me sane as you hold me

blessed are the poor
blessed is the poor man's faith
blessed are the scars
blessed is my Savior's face

dreaming your kingdom come
what would our hearts be like
dreaming your will be done
though part of me fights it

dreaming, too, these earthbound needs
yet not by bread alone
humbly approach your throne
yet running to you, freely

you meant for me to dream
while I listened to the
lies whispering only
the broken need anything

is hope really poor man's faith
like they always told me
'cause faith, hope, and love keep
me sane as you hold me

blessed are the poor
blessed is the poor man's faith

•

1 Cor. 13:13

GIFTS + GRACE

Hope has always been a tough one. "Just believe and God will say yes" can assume an awful lot. That we can always know what he's thinking. That he's limited to one form of expression. That he deals with us as if there are no stages of development, plotlines bigger than us, or other kinds of blessings and messages. That he has just one way of meeting us.

Is it a sign that God cares for you more or is more active in your life if you have a spouse, a house, and at least a couple of kids? If your body heals in ways all the doctors said couldn't happen? If yours was the house that was spared when the rest of the neighborhood was leveled by a wildfire? If another round of layoffs took more from your group and you're one of the few left? If you've always got a smile on your face? If your faith makes you popular rather than a target?

What about the rest of us?

What about blessed are the poor, those who mourn, and the persecuted? For theirs is the kingdom, the comfort, and some of the greatest rewards heaven has to give.

I've begun to see how God uses every last thing this world can throw at us to show us his heart. He's a master storyteller who loves and sees the poor of this world. To whatever kind of poor that might be he says, "Come to me."

As jaded as I've gotten with such blanket "God always does A, B, or C" formulaic statements, and with my passion about how I've seen God move through harder things, I have to check myself now and then so I don't fall into the trap of overcorrecting. We're told to hope. We're told to come to God with our requests, with expectancy, and to keep on asking. We're told to ask big, and the bigger the better.

Not one of us is exempt from this. It's not just for those we've identified as the go-to gifted in healing, hearing from God, teaching, and leading. May I just suggest there's a difference between asking or even moving in authority and attempting to force God's hand.

In some things, certain people are particularly gifted. "Gift" being the operative root despite how it's stretched her or him. And when something's become second nature and our grid for moving with God, it's easy to start putting those expectations on others. Even resenting that more aren't as focused on the same thing or as bold in its wielding. Forgetting the gift of it, or the downright anointing. Forgetting that the part of the body we are differs from others by design.

How and why God gives, withholds, and develops his gifts is a whole different conversation. A compelling one, and I'm certain the things I don't know there outnumber the things I understand. If we were God, we'd open the whole shop up—take what you want whenever you want because it's all good stuff, right? But he distributes these things as he sees fit. Differing gifts we're all invited—even urged—to ask for, and some given to certain people in greater or more consistent measure.

I have a few thoughts about why that might be, but I could be wrong. One thing from my vantage point, though, seems like a fair observation. If a specific gift becomes our barometer for determining God's activity or goodness, it just might be an idol we're clinging to rather than Jesus. Every single good thing he gives us has that potential.

When it comes to his gifts, we can and should ask him for some of the biggies. But what about the lesser ones?

It's from a point of weakness that I say this, but when I read all of 1 Corinthians 12, that doesn't sound quite so bad.

> On the contrary, those parts of the body that seem to
> be weaker are indispensable... (1 Cor. 12:22 NIV)

One day a physical therapist helping me with the pain running through my jaw, neck, back, and shoulders explained that my larger muscles were so strong and solid, but the crippling pain preventing movement was because the smaller ones were stressed. They could no longer handle being driven by the larger muscles' plans. He prescribed micromovements as a way to begin finding my way back to wholeness.

It frustrates me to have to change what I'm doing. I used to be able to do these things just fine, but now something's slowing me down. I've had to take a fresh look at that whole doing-versus-being disconnect. Inviting the whole body back into the conversation.

Mission at the expense of the body. We all know that sounds wrong, but we all know we kind of do it. Come to think of it, I'm probably doing it again right now—been running on fumes all week, pushing it, and I should probably put down this pen. My shoulders can take just so much time in this position.

You know when some guys spend all their time in the gym working their upper bodies but don't bother with their legs? What looks impressive in a selfie or with the right clothing can end up looking, bless their hearts, a little funky from a different angle. Some churches skip leg day, and muscles are walking around on toothpicks. Not always because of inherent weakness but because of a lack of equal focus and respect.

Sometimes there's what we as a community, as a body, want others to see and what we want to be known for, but then there's who we actually are together and the parts that make up a whole different picture. Vision is necessary—it's the tunnel vision that gets us into trouble.

We've gotten so far from what God intended for us to live out. Whether we know it or not, we all need each other.

Weakness needs strength, clearly. But sometimes even strength needs to hear—really hear—another story: In my weakness he is strong, and God's grace really is sufficient.

•

Even faith is a gift.

> For through the grace given to me I say to everyone among you not to think more highly of himself than he ought to think; but to think so as to have sound judgment, as God has allotted to each a measure of faith. (Rom. 12:3 NASB)

I can't even do that much without God's help. And after all this time I can still be clumsy in its wielding. For all my certainty, there's still that challenge to grow in faith. Stepping out and waiting will never be entirely easy.

Hope is that thing in us that dares to ask. That dares to ask for the strength to ask. How much do I dare even want? How much of that risk can my heart handle?

Who's to say which kind of hope takes more strength—bigger hope in the face of a confidence in yes, or any hope at all in the face of a potential no or not yet. And it only takes faith the size of a mustard seed to move mountains. Be strong, be brave, he says to the seed falling to the ground with a softness that shakes a mountain down to its foundations.

There are times God gives me the strongest promptings that defy all my reasoning and urges me to battle in prayer, song, and action and, sure enough, I've seen the seas part in hearts, bodies, and circumstances. But to me, that's a little more like faith. It's easier when you've got that heads-up that you're invited into something he's already doing.

But how do I pray and live and hope when God is a little more silent and the answers are more hidden? When they're my own desires that I'm bringing to him? When faced with my own uncertainties, how do I hope in the face of not knowing? When waiting begins to feel like a no, and I'm not sure at what point I should consider it my answer and switch gears?

•

Father, your Son is my defense. He's all I have to boast about. He's my present, my future, my hope. Still, this is no stoic, ascetic life devoid of all wanting. And my spiritual life doesn't play out in a vacuum. There's no sacred-secular divide in my longings. You don't make your home in just half of my heart.

Here are my desires. All of them. The ones I've talked to you about a hundred times before and the ones I haven't brought up at all. Some of those I've been trying to meet my own way, and some I'd rather not look at too closely because it's such a risk to want them too much.

You don't just see what I want, you see through all the layers to the roots. That's what I bring before you. Answer more perfectly than I even know to ask for.

Search me and know me. You know what's moving in me even if I don't. You know what's crying to be born in and through and around me. There's no name I can say out loud yet, but it's a life I want to see and hold.

Still, I bring you, too, some real specifics. These things I'm hoping for above all others in this season. Some things I can and some things I can't even work toward much less control. These things I can only watch and wait for. I don't know what I'll do if they don't come about. And so I don't only ask for these things, I ask for what's going on in me as I walk through the waiting. In expectancy I'm watching to see how all this will play out, hoping in you and trusting.

This is confidence speaking now, but I know I need something more. I can do confidence, and I can do surrender, but I can't yet perfectly walk out the balance of them together. Only you can do this in me.

•

Ps. 38:9, Matt. 17:20, 1 Cor. 12, 1 Pet. 4:10

BELIEVE WITH YOU

blessed are the never been kissed
believing love's around the corner
blessed are the hands unheld
open for the receiving

blessed are the standing alone
whose strength is tried in season
blessed are the wanderers
with reasons to keep going on

I'm gonna believe with you
may God's face shine upon you

blessed, oh, are the hope deferred
believing their answers are coming
the ones who stand, heads held high
while shaking faces ask them why

blessed are the starting over
and the ones who have yet to begin
blessed are those who get up
when they hear God's voice calling them

I'm gonna believe with you
may God's face shine upon you

HOLD CLOSER

I've held hope at bay
because the past laughs "no"
I've pushed peace away
because of what my eyes behold

but you don't kick covers off
because the day is cold
you hold them closer
you dive deeper
you stay longer
than on an ordinary day

HILLS + HANDPRINTS

Roadtrips have always been heaven. The drive just as much as the arriving. When I was a kid, my parents and brother and I would take off in the van for the summer. For up to a couple months we'd explore all over the country. We'd drive from national park to extended family visit, to rented fishing cabin, to campsite, to wherever my dad would need to teach for a week. We'd wait there for him then continue our loop. By my teens I'd set foot on nearly every state in the lower forty-eight. Most of them many times over.

Long before cellphones and movies you could take anywhere, all we had all those miles were books, music, writing, talking, scenery, and thinking. It was more than enough. I rarely got bored. The more time the better, lost in my thoughts.

On those open stretches I'd stare for hours at the land and skies. Picturing it all without the black asphalt that drew a winding line punctuated with signs, a string of dots and dashes speaking a different story.

I'd imagine Native American villages, explorers seeing all of this for the first time, and what it would feel like to be a settler or a pioneer leaving everything familiar behind.

Traveling in a day what had once taken others weeks or months, I'd feel both adventurous and apprehensive about the magnitude of what rides on our stories. And about what it can be like for stories to collide. Not all the tales had been sanitized, romanticized, simplified. I knew how much blood had been shed here and why. In my mind's eye, enemies would have been friends and we would have found a way to live together. Maybe we should let kids try running things for a while. Though, no—in time, school hadn't proven much different in its own ways.

My favorite sights were hills and mountains where the land starts to crunch higher and higher into the sky from acts of destruction and creation that I always tried to picture. Tectonic plates pressing against each other, the force pushing land up and down. Just how much had this land shaken, and how often? Just how much force would have to be behind a connection that moves land this far away? The science of all those plates shifting, not to mention populations migrating over time, blew my mind. Endless fascination. How did we all get to where we came from?

At the same time, though, the peaks looked like knuckles and the slopes stemming from them looked like fingers, and I smiled to think of God kneading the earth like bread. His handprints were everywhere. Somehow I knew God was both scientist and artist. There's no equation for the endless variety of beauty he thought up and fashioned, the way the sight of it affects our pulse and respiration, and how it all says something about him.

That's the kind of time I grew up spending with God. Seeing him everywhere, and my heart writing him love songs every time I saw his signature.

And the church I was raised in was big on teaching and studying. Nerd alert—in my early teens I was even on a Bible quiz team. Shut up, I loved it. I'm grateful for those years of poring over the Bible and learning what's there. I could write a decent report when that came up.

We focused on other things, too. Yes, there at church, but emphasized and twisted in increasingly broken ways at home.

I'm still not entirely sure when the focus on learning shifted into a lifestyle of correction and a fear of being found out as less than perfect. Or when I started to break under the weight of it all.

I'm still not sure when church went from a place of freedom and joy to one of fear of not living up to expectations, and fear of breaking the code of silence. No different than the world in this way, from my vantage point, there were things you just didn't talk about and appearances to keep up—not to mention competitiveness among those in business. Religion doesn't have a monopoly on this but, for us, silence and hiding harder realities were sanctified by the obligation to be a proper witness for Jesus. That witness came to mean image rather than honesty.

Church became the place where I had to stop crying and plaster on a smile, rather than the place I could go with my deep well of tears. In our family in particular, to reveal cracks in the image threatened catastrophe.

I'm still not sure when grace was put on the shelf like a decorative platter rather than one for daily serving, or when life in action almost solely began to emphasize the will.

We were taught to share the gospel in scripted ways that, even thinking about them, left me feeling like a high-pressure salesman. And I hadn't even begun to make my quota yet. There were certain ways I just couldn't bring myself to speak to other people. Like God was beachfront property and I was a realtor explaining the contract in jargon.

And sin and repentance, like love, were emphasized, but in a way that weaponized them. Shattering reverie, repercussions for anything and everything struck without warning like a lightning storm on a cloudless, sunny morning. A disconnect that was always hard to reconcile.

It all took its toll, and I began to mistrust my instincts and my own thoughts.

"I'm sorry," I prayed, even when I wasn't sure what I'd done wrong. "I'll be better," I promised God, though the thread of what that meant was already lost. Slips of the tongue, some even parroted, met consequences that left me crying, hiding behind the door I wasn't allowed to lock. The door shaking as hard as me at the fist pounding on it.

Unable to predict what I shouldn't do or say or what else might trigger contempt or rage, eventually I broke the code. I started noticing some things. Now and then I'd said something insightful or right, not realizing it was dangerous to observe or know too much. Or I'd gotten hurt, making me both clumsy and costly. And when I was made to feel foolish, it was because I'd let a corner of my heart slip out that didn't mirror those around me closely enough.

It wasn't so much that I was wrong about something but that I was wrong inherently. In ways others didn't seem to be. There was no way to be small enough, but I tried my best.

Once broken, love withdrawn and given was to me like pulls and slack on horse's reigns, like pressing heels, like spurs, and steered me daily with subtleties more than enough.

Safety came in silence. In doing what I was told. In repeating the right answers without probing them, at least out loud. In anticipating others' needs and getting ahead of any request or demand. In being unseen and left alone. In filling required roles. In devouring books and movies. In living out what I needed within my imagination.

I journaled and wrote poetry, then shredded every last page. Certain the content was more proof that I was ridiculous.

I found ways to hurt myself that were invisible to others just to try to relieve some of the weight. Though I walked around smiling.

I found a careful way to be that no longer worked when it came time to move out. Needing to go from childhood to adulthood without having experienced a real adolescence, I'm sure that must have been entertaining for some to watch. Some turned even crueler once they found out how much I could take, like it was a fun game to find my breaking point.

Everyone on all sides pulled the reigns now, and in dozens of different directions. Knowing the ensuing dichotomies could only be further evidence of my worthlessness and wrongness, it was more than I could take. I was so alone, and the running list of why that must be kept growing.

But in the middle of all that fresh new chaos, I started hearing something else. Quiet, but standing out because of the contrast in tone.

"This is wrong."

Those words rose up in my spirit. I'd heard them before over the years, but this time they were louder. Stronger. More distinct. And I realized that they were defending me.

> The Lord is close to the brokenhearted and saves those
> who are crushed in spirit. (Ps. 34:18 NIV)

This right here, this was the same God I still sang to and knew and loved. The same God I believed in. This was one of so many verses that always made my spirit do backflips. These were things that, deep down, I knew were true. Something in me was testifying to it. Loving, compassionate, I knew this was God's heart. I knew he was this way. I guess I'd disqualified myself a long time ago, thinking verses like this applied to others, not myself.

What if those words could come off the page and be more real to me? Not just to my mind, but to my actual life.

I was twenty-three when it dawned on me that there could be another kind of a conversation with God. And that maybe he could help with what I was up against in life and within myself.

I bought a new spiral notebook and pen and went to a picnic table in the middle of a park's green expanse. Though I could just as well have spoken it, and in my spirit I did, I began a letter to God just to help get my thoughts in order and start the conversation. I often think better through the end of my pen. And I found myself praying the most transforming prayer I'd prayed since that very first one at five: God, help me trust you.

I'd read about how God leads and guides. I'd read how he answers prayers. I'd read how the things he speaks happen. And there was no question I'd loved him and he'd loved me all those years. But this time when I prayed, I was desperate for some kind of change. I needed an answer to live out. I needed to know he still writes these stories. I needed to trust him—not in general, but for my life. And not just for the ending, but for every single day. I put my life in his hands in a new way. I took him at his word and called him on everything I'd heard about him.

After years of quiet growing, something more was now happening. The land in me began to shift. Like those mountains, sometimes so much at once and other times bit by bit.

Looking back now I can almost picture God rolling up his sleeves with a smile of inspiration. This would be no sketch, no weekend project. This would be a piece of art he'd invest in and finish. Broad strokes and intricate details no other artist would have thought of.

•

I wish I could say it's been easy. You know, all the happily-ever-afters so many spiritual appeals rest on. And the thing is, with many it really does work that way, to a degree. Sudden freedom all at once after a lifetime of suffering or walking in a different direction. Journeys every bit as powerful and valid and I celebrate with them. But I lost years of my life comparing myself to them.

For me, it's taken a lifetime just to get here. Are there things to mourn? Sure, and I have, and I do now and then. And yet this is no consolation prize I'm holding—this freedom and joy in Jesus. This life is just a fraction of eternity. Is anything I've missed out on really greater than what I've come out of this with?

Still, there's often this look of skepticism that Jesus is enough—even in the eyes of some who, holding their other treasures, make the same claim. The conversation can get frustrating when some of us are speaking different languages.

"Trust in what?" is a clarifying question when we talk about our hopes and dreams in this life. Trust that God will meet my agenda or that I'm safe within his? That God will give me what I want or that he'll meet my deepest needs? That he'll answer the way I think he should or show me he'll meet me no matter what?

Sometimes those instantly freed are the ones who challenge us to trust bigger and trust for more. But sometimes it's us. Members of the Long Road and Hard Answers Club.

The mountains, with their layers exposed, remind me of all the time and history that have gone into their beauty.

> And Jesus answered saying to them, "Have faith in God. Truly I say to you, whoever says to this mountain, 'Be taken up and cast into the sea,' and does not doubt in his heart, but believes that what he says is going to happen, it will be granted him. Therefore I say to you, all things for which you pray and ask, believe that you have received them, and they will be granted you." (Mark 11:22-24 NASB)

Why is this always used as an example of instant answers? How could there be time or room for either doubt or faith if it were always as simple as one experience? You'd better believe I can have huge hope, faith, and trust for five minutes or even twenty-four hours. But some answers take moments, and others seasons, lifetimes, or generations.

My story is not what everyone will or even should experience. It's just that so many put that instant, microwave expectation out there that others walking a longer road within certain circles can end up short on encouragement. To put it mildly. The well-meaning faithful undermining their expectations and faith, sometimes on a weekly basis.

Been there. For years I left impassioned prayer sessions, way too many to count, more beaten up and despairing than lifted up. It felt like attempts to dig up my roots to expose them to sunlight out of impatience for the blossoms. Internally I went away limping.

Every time it happened, it would take time to recover from that kind of caring. Jesus and I in my lonely place's garden, on our knees, handful by handful carefully putting my soul's soil back in place. The Holy Spirit himself the water bearer, speaking to stones. Telling me to soften, not harden, from it all.

It makes sense why this subject makes for such strong reactions. You see God move in such a big way and naturally want everyone to get a taste of that very same thing. How can we go for it in prayer and yet not squelch everything else the Spirit might want to do? All glory to God and his prolific, multilingual storytelling. He humbles our models and preferences and expectations and expands our perspectives. If we let him, that is.

I'm still enrolled in this school. The tension between hope, faith, and mystery, and between yes, no, and waiting, it isn't easy, and it never quite lets up. But, oh, what I've seen him do with my trust.

I still don't know what tomorrow will bring. What other blessings will or won't be gained or lost in this life. What challenges are or aren't ahead that God might walk me through differently than I'd have chosen. Like some of these other things he's already redeemed to the point that I'd have been less without them, as odd as that sounds.

I couldn't always say this, but I do trust his heart toward me. And I trust that his imagination, plans, and purposes are greater than mine.

Some days I can even see the mountains moving.

If we don't cry out "blessed is he," the stones will.

•

Acts 1:8, Rom. 1:20, Rom. 12:12, 2 Cor. 3:2-3, 2 Cor. 3:18, 1 Pet. 3:15

A CRY ON THE WIND

I'm a grain of sand
a star, a cry on the wind
and yet you call my name
and yet you take my hand

The tides and heavens
and winds obey your commands
and they move me to dance
and move me to praise you

God Almighty, you made the oceans
and you have numbered our tears
What kind of God loves like you love
You're the Lion, the Lamb, the Holy One
and I'm in awe of you

God of the expanse
and God of the multitudes
You're Lord of my own heart
breath of life to my soul

•

Gen. 13:16, Gen. 15:5

OPEN DOOR

I feel the breeze on my face
from an open door
from a way you've made
turning this way and that to find it
arms stretched high like a question
    like a cry
        like a prayer

and wide like an answer
    like a smile
        like flying free to somewhere

what's clearer today is the light that's still there
how else could there be such long
shadows at this time of day
however did I miss it

something got in the way
something's been hiding your face
something's stolen my gaze

listing the lies letting go
easier to breathe
easier to see
not abandoned, Lord
and still believing in seeds

CHERYL VELK

GOLGOTHA

At the place where Jesus was crucified,
there was a garden,
and in the garden a new tomb,
in which no one had ever been laid.
(John 19:41 NIV)

CHERYL VELK

chapter nine

CLIFFHANGER

DAWNING GRACE

that Maybe-Future of the Guarded Hope shines
like a morse code candle flickering in and out of view
leaving me to read the in-between
and wonder which speaks
the light or the darkness
the inhale or the exhale

that Fragile Dark of the Dawning Grace meets
its fate again and again with the
faintest glimmering dots and dashes
reading a swelling song to aching, doubting throats
revealing the darkness weaker
so fully conquered by something so small

A BIGGER TALE TO TELL

Whatever else pain is or is not, it's a force that shapes us. There are tools of demolition, construction, and artistry within our waiting. Within our lament and praise. Within our questioning and seeking.

God knew full well what, along with his hands, had worked together to form me. He knew my clay. And rather than just shaking his head, moving on to material less trouble and more easily worked, he stayed. While I just saw my mess, like a true artist he saw the possibilities.

Miracles come on all scales. God is the God of both the micro and the macro. He's the God of both the instant and the laboriously epic trilogy. A thousand years is like a day to him, and forty years a blink.

Sometimes the cliffhanger lasts three days or one breath-caught moment. Sometimes it's a test result, a phone call, a bill, a fleece. And sometimes it seems we're on the edge of our seats perpetually. Fighting, hanging on by our fingernails, or sheltering in place where we feel most safe for years or even decades. How are we going to get out of this one? Or will we?

I've known rescue and relief by nightfall even while I've labored through years of challenge and suspense. There've been both manna and feasts within seasons of enduring.

Somehow on the other side of all this wrestling and in the midst of this intertwining Good Friday, Holy Saturday and Easter morning, I find in myself a spirit of expectancy that was once beyond me.

•

It's always hard to talk specifics about your challenges and hardest seasons, knowing that anyone, comparing their own, could be thinking anything from "how horrifying, I'm so glad it's not me" to "how mild, how sad, how silly; she should see my list."

This whole past decade, really, was about taking care of business no matter what the cost. I'd finally reached the end of my reasoning and strength. My ways had been exhausted; they'd had their chance. The hamster wheel in my head went to the curb, along with everything I'd thought I needed, and I asked God to show me something new. And no half-measures—if we were going to do all this, I wanted him to tackle it all at my roots.

There was a lot I still wanted. A lot I still needed. But this was about surrender of my agenda. Abandonment to his timeline and ways and ultimate ends. I handed him the life I'd been holding on to so tightly.

Take up your cross daily, Jesus said, and follow me. Lose your life and you'll find it, he said. He died for us, but will we die to self?

Father, if there's any other way let this cup pass from me, but your will be done no matter what.

Jesus said a tear-choked yes, and so do we. And after that yes there often comes a long, hard walk.

The Via Dolorosa—the Way of Grief, the Way of Sorrow, the Painful Way—leads to a place of a type of death. But it's the very same place that can lead to victory, resurrection, and the deepest, most genuine joy.

Why was this my road to walk? The question slowly faded as I began to find myself in possession of things more crucial than answers.

What seemed like a lifetime of growth and healing was squeezed into a few years. There was no anesthesia or Novocain during all that surgery on my thinking, but I got through it. And some of the most precious friendships of my life were forged in the fires of those years.

But then it got physical, and God made it clear that there would be no stopping short of the finish line when it came to what he had in mind—something I still couldn't picture.

This was no easy choice. This yes on top of the last one would ultimately cost about a decade of my life. It took a while to grieve that and come to terms with what I wanted most out of life. The time was going to pass anyway—once it did, where did I want to be? After much deliberation I shook my head at myself, saying, "Future Me is going to owe me big-time," and with my voice shaking, I told God okay.

Step one was the family feet, an issue since well before even my teens. Heredity and time had done their thing. Major reconstruction was needed to get out of the hobbling pain I faced by the end of each day, and best to do it younger while the best options were still on the table. It took three major surgeries in one year, complete with four months on crutches and more time in walking boots, and endless physical therapy.

Support seemed to materialize out of thin air. Both friends and strangers kept reaching out in their own individual ways. A dinner brought over, an hour of conversation, dishes washed, rugs vacuumed, a run to a grocery store for a dollar-fifty item. A door held open, a hand steadying me from falling, bags carried from my trunk to my top steps. Dozens and dozens of small things over the course of the year all speaking worth and caring. I kid you not, it was Valentine's Day when the penny dropped, and I realized the whole past year had been a love letter from God. He'd used everyone—and everything—to spend the whole year saying "I love you" and "you have worth." Each person going out of their way, with me unable to remove the cost of myself from the interaction. It took experiencing it that many times for it to sink deeper than the lies.

While I was still limping, I turned to face the even bigger deal. Like the feet, this also started way back in childhood but had finally gotten to the point that I could no longer take it. It was a bite misaligned with the pain now working its way through more of my body in a chain reaction. Neck, shoulders, arms, back—everything.

This had also started as a matter of heredity, and time played a role. But so had doctors. My entire teen years were spent in braces, and I'd been abandoned in shape just about as bad as I'd started out in. Over the next couple decades, doctor after doctor—some limited, some dismissive—promised to help but made things even more of a sick joke. My body, it seemed, was not my own. Give them your money and don't challenge these experts. Just sit there and listen to the lectures, like I'd done all this to myself.

While I'd generally learned what I was in for at the same time as the feet—all those initial appointments had been held at the same time—my core dental team of four doctors did even more involved evaluations once I was ready to go. After they met to discuss my case, it fell to one of them to give me the big picture.

It was one of the more complex cases they'd seen, and the road ahead would be unusually rough, involved, and expensive. To the degree that she encouraged me to seriously consider whether getting no care at all might be easier to take. None of the easier, quicker options would work, and it was an all or nothing sort of situation. This would take at least five years. They needed to be sure I was all in.

Hearing that was devastating because the pain was intolerable. I hadn't been able to sleep on my side for the previous six months, movement was getting more and more limited, and pain just kept getting worse.

It's hard to overstate the emotional and psychological weight of risking handing myself back over to these doctors. I can still remember sitting in my car outside a couple of these offices at the start of this journey, crying my eyes out and praying for courage and hope. And because people go through some of these things, and more, every day without that intense of a reaction, it was obvious that it wasn't just about the physical process to come. It was all rubbing up against a whole lot of raw and bruised and misused places in me. Places where I was afraid and in need of hope, strength, and things I couldn't yet see well enough to name.

•

Awake during one of the surgeries, it was my sweet periodontist who I heard sigh, scalpel in hand, "Oh, Cheryl. Everything you've been through. And you didn't deserve any of it." Earlier I'd prayed, "God, please be my physician," and it was like those words had been said by both of them, in unison. It was one of many moments of healing that went way past physical.

It's been six years straight now of being under construction and all-in. Countless specialists and appointments and not a single day off the potter's wheel.

Most days it's felt like climbing a mountain, just needing to keep putting one foot in front of the other—and that's made me stronger and forged endurance. Some days it's felt like chrysalis time, with quiet days of quiet healing and perseverance and perspective—and that's made me calmer and more trusting and more present in the moment. Many turbulent days it's taken a ridiculous amount of fighting and speaking up for myself and within myself—and that's made me freer and more whole.

It's also been six years of so many people trying to pray this entire path away for me. While yes, I'd have bawled with relief had I not had to deal with such a hard road, and I have seen with my own eyes God heal people instantly and fully, it was one of those times where I knew that I knew, deep in my spirit, that I needed to walk through this. And because I somehow knew such love and wisdom were behind it, I said yes. Though it was one of the hardest yeses I've ever said.

I am so grateful for those rare few who heard me when I explained the myriad ways God was meeting me within the journey. Revealing his faithfulness and goodness, showing me what it's like to lean on his strength at the end of my own, filling me with deep joy and peace in the midst of the unlikeliest circumstances, exercising certain muscles of heart and mind and spirit, freeing and healing me from past traumas (medical and otherwise), and pointing out different things in my heart that needed handing over to him. And how I believed he'd let me know in no uncertain terms at the outset that a long, hard road was ahead and that I just needed to trust him.

I am so grateful for these friends who've walked with me, and who so many times just sat with me within the mystery of all God was working out within me. With these persistent physical issues throughout my teens and well on into adulthood, all within the context of everything else going on in life and different formative situations and incidents along the way, it all got knit into the fabric of who I was. Those just aren't threads—knots—that you can untangle in a day. It's felt like the quick-fixers, despite their good intentions, were doing violence to that every single time. The internal transformation has far exceeded the physical, and there has just been no rushing that. He's answered those prayers for healing—just not in the way everyone has expected to see.

That Joseph reached the end of his years of betrayals and unfair consequences softened rather than hardened was a grace as great as God's sovereignty in saving his people from famine through him. Not all struggle comes with such a clear ending or reason that satisfies. And yet, still, God promises beauty for ashes. And yet, still, God promises that all things work together for good for those who love him and are called according to his purpose.

•

Isn't it tempting to wait until we reach the end to tell a story? I almost waited. Even now there's further to go, and I still don't know quite where I'll wind up. And, yes, I'm praying that God would intervene. But the whole point is that it's right here in this uncertain place that I'm able to say, with all my heart, "God is so faithful and so good." No cliché in that—been living and celebrating the magnitude of those words for a long while now. It's no trite greeting card statement.

So many loved ones are walking unbelievably rough roads of various kinds that they don't have the luxury of seeing a finish line for. And this may never be fully over for me. This is real life with all its messiness and ups and downs and unpredictability and losses. And the reality of God's presence and goodness has nothing to do with getting everything we want. It's he himself that ends up being enough.

He's the prize. My pearl of great price, worth everything. It's not like the jury is out on his goodness and faithfulness until I see what the end of this particular road looks like. He's good today. He's faithful today. He's how I ever got this far in the first place. And because of that I know I can handle tomorrow, whatever it brings.

I know he's heard my prayers. But not just today's saying, "Rescue me." Just one of many prayers I prayed before that was, "God, help me trust you." How precious, even if sometimes bittersweet, to finally be on the same page about which is the greater thing.

•

Gen. 50:19-20, Dan. 3:16-18, Ps. 105:17-20, Matt. 16:24-25, Mark 8:34-35, Luke 14:27, Rom. 8:28

ALL HALLOW'S EVE

the dry leaf cracked like a communion cup
as it passed from my hand

with a soft snap I let go of what had fallen
and something in me gave way

one must be born again, one must be made new
one must let go of what had been

GRAVES

Lord, what am I supposed to do in a place like this? I know the right answer on the quiz, but I need to hear your voice again. I know you're good. You've proven that over and over. But so much happens in this life that is so not okay. So much that's exhausting and takes us over and over again past the end of ourselves. And lately my heart's had a bunch of square-one moments.

Square one—see how I talk to myself about this? As if it's possible to learn or grow our way past needing to deal with pain, grief, anger, confusion. As if to fall apart means somehow to fall backwards. There is no knowing better than this when mourning comes. It's a common stretch of road we don't get to bypass.

Grief and confusion can make you feel like a beginner at life and faith again. A child. Not the woman or man you thought you'd become.

After five years of this exhausting, expensive, ridiculously involved dental battle, today I should be feeling "finished." But recent days and weeks have hit snags that have brought me to tears of grief, helplessness, and frustration. There's perspective, there's so much to be grateful for— where I am is no horrible place, and it was such grace to have had the luxury of even getting this far. I'm just really, really tired. So much time, pain, expense, vigilance, fear, and anticipation have gone into all this.

Of course, I chastised myself for what I thought of as my emotional overreaction to my current state. One good, solid, fleeting funk should have been enough, right? A couple movies in my pj's, snacking on all the wrong things, a good cry, and boom, done. We all need that once in a while.

It took me a few days to recognize that this deep well of grief was about more than teeth. It was the chance the grief of the world had to pour through this breach in the dam of my carefully, rationally spoken to feelings. Were I to mourn every conversation, headline, and situation, and the magnitude of ongoing need around me, to the depth it deserves, Lord, I'd never get out of bed again. Boundaries, right? But even boundaries can overflow their banks. There's just so much perspective our hearts can take before they break open, too full of all the building expression they've been denied.

Barring another miracle yet to be seen—God, please, I believe you can still stun us all one more time with unexpected reprieve—after four years of beating all odds time and time again, one of my dearest friends now appears to be losing her battle with cancer. At the very least, her remaining options have never been this slim. And with others I care about, almost daily there are new words in our conversations like ultrasound, funeral, mastectomy, layoff, separation, divorce, natural disaster, injury, financial stress, mental illness, politics, suicide, struggling children, struggling parents, relational rifts. Rocks and hard places, and everyone and everything stuck in between them.

Any other month and this dental plot twist would not have been the single hailstone that shattered my heart's glass. Any other month and this would not have been the one stone dislodged from a dam that made the wall breach and wreak havoc upon my lonely place.

Beneath my cries of "it's not fair" hides the subtext: My God, my God, why have you forsaken me? Where are you? I can't see a thing through all these tears.

If only we could show up at a gravesite after three days, like Mary did to yours, Lord, and see that one we love standing there smiling at us. Instead we go to graves both literal and figurative, and they're still haunted by the memories of the people and things we've lost. Instead of an angel saying, "The One you're looking for is alive," we pick up a phone, go through a door, reach out instinctively, and we feel again the weight of the silence and absence. Not your silence, not the absence of you, but of the things and ones we've lost.

We look at the calendar and are reminded of time lost, paths taken, and the impossibility of a do-over. We look at ourselves and our lives, and there are injustices beyond bearing. Sometimes even just through more of a chain reaction of circumstances or ignorance or fallibility than any malice. Still, there are thieves we name as we grieve and try to forgive for the seventieth-times-seventh time. Others. Ourselves. The world. Things unseen. So many passionate cries for justice won't stop until Jesus returns.

How long, O Lord.

For those of us who love and trust you we know we'll be reunited. We know one day every wrong thing will be made right. And we're told this life's deepest losses and injuries will feel like momentary, light affliction in comparison to all the joy that's waiting for us. But you can believe all the right things and still need to grieve. Right here, right now, we have to take action and fight and keep the faith. We have to go on. And there is so much legitimate sorrow.

It's within this not-quite-yet that we wrestle and yearn and once in a great while on an empty stretch of highway even the quietest among us take advantage of the privacy and scream our hearts out into the dark. That was me a few nights ago, for a good hour. The night before, driving that same road, the skies had raged in a furious downpour with chain lightning far too close like I'd never seen before, shaking me to my core, as if to say you, God, can handle the contents of my poured-out, unleashed heart. They're not too big for you to bear. Not too wild to scare you away. And as if to pour out a taste of your own heart, too. One of the ways in which you say, "I know. I know."

It's easy for me to forget how your anger gets kindled on my behalf, the Father that you are. How your face isn't blank in response to my anguish. How your compassion for this state is what prompted the greatest sacrifice anyone's ever made. Your Son. The cross. Your love. Your grace.

Your tenderness is a wilder thing than expected within this raging storm in me, Lord. It doesn't just express itself in quiet moments. I've felt your steady strength, your stillness, within my most out of control places. An active, powerful kind of anchoring. No amount of my internal chaos can tear me from you or drown out your saying my name. And nothing will ever steal your praise from my lips.

Jesus Christ is Lord. Over my hope. Over my fear. Over my grief. Over my joy. Over my confusion. Over my sin. Over my misunderstanding. Over my complaints. Over my gratitude. Over my longing. Over my dancing. Over my fists pressed to my eyes flooded with tears, my body rocked with my fiercest extremes. Jesus Christ is Lord.

Over my questions. Over my learning curve. Over my weakness. Over my strength. Over my perseverance. Over my falling, and falling again. Over my getting back up to my feet.

Lord, I believe. Help my unbelief.

In your compassion and mercy, you find me where I've run to and hidden.

You find me walking down a road and join in my conversation, smiling when on my face you finally see my look of recognition.

I carry spices to my garden's graves, half blind with tears, love the only kind of strength I have left. You find me there and remind me of all the life, in you, beyond them.

•

Luke 24:32, John 19:41-42, John 20:11-16, John 20:19

BATTLECRY LAMENT

I'm holding on to this idea that this is foundation building time and God is drawing me into something new with what I've had to persevere through lately. And again tonight.

I'm holding on to the idea that God's been using so much this year to teach me—to show me—something about strength and prayer and power.

But tonight, once again I just feel so weak and in need of help. Rescue, protection. It's hard to go there in prayer today, tonight, because I just want to scream and cry out for God to save my friends in and through and from their battles. I just want to grieve and rage for friends who've endured so much for so long.

I want to shout this shaking, bellowing, straight from my gut, soul-shaking cry of "enough" at every demon on its way to hell that devotes its pathetic, cursed, irredeemable excuse for an existence to tormenting me and those I love, and grieving the heart of God. May God himself rebuke each and every one of them.

I want to scream "enough" to my Father God, my Abba, my Daddy, and watch life and limb and minds and hearts and circumstances transform in a wave of grace and mercy as God himself repeats that word "enough" and unleashes holy hell in the unseen on all those tormentors and liars and tricksters and imprisoners.

I want to call God on every promise, and by every name he goes by— Wonderful Counselor, Mighty God, Everlasting Father, Prince of Peace, protector, provider, healer, righteous judge, merciful, full of grace, the Most High, Elohim, God of Justice, the God Who is Near, the God of Truth, the God who comes to make the blind see and the lame walk and the deaf hear, the God who is compassionate and heals both body and soul, the God who frees captives, and the God who restores and reconciles. It is this God, the God of Abraham, Isaac, and Jacob, who I call out to in the precious, holy name of Jesus. God, enough.

I know all too well that the Bible doesn't promise smooth seas and clear pathways. But it does promise us power in the name of Jesus and the hand of God Almighty at work in the most personal ways. It does promise that he works all things out, ultimately, for our good and his glory.

Father God, I'm asking for maximum transformation. I'm asking for repayment for all the enemy has stolen. I'm asking that the name of Jesus be glorified in and through our lives. I'm asking for your light to shine all the brighter in every dark place, and to fully conquer that darkness. And I'm asking for radical, miraculous, compassionate responses to these specific circumstances, to these specific requests, to these specific heart cries. Fight for us.

•

Ps. 138:3,8

LETTING GO

Lord, all I hold on to
that I'm meant to hand to you
all these heavy things and souls
lifted tonight like carbonated butterflies
through an opening you made
released to your care
which was the whole point
in the first place
I almost forgot to let go
of myself, too
the last one to fly, I flew

chapter ten

UNEARTHED

A MEMORY ON GRANDMA'S BIRTHDAY

what did you have at the Cantonese place
Grandma would ask our grandfather
number thirteen, he'd answer
his face straight as a pin but
smiling inside as her fist
flew to her hip—
you really make that live
half laugh, half prim
her high-heeled toe would tap

solitaire with a silky snap, snap, snap
gentle at the kitchen table
shapes and faces patiently
turned to hers
until she gathered them into their sleeve
standing and announcing
I'm going to go upstairs to start a fight
with your grandfather
Grandma!
well, it keeps him hanging on

you look sixteen to me
he gently took her hand
we never heard her answer
from that rolling bed in the family room
where the sofa had been
no tap, tap
no snap, snap
just a look in his eyes I'd never seen before
and fighting was never fun again

CAVERNS + COLORS

My thoughts tallying losses like a needle guiding embroidery thread, in and out, weaving patterns and pictures in my stillness, I take this cloth out of that drawer in my spirit as I thread a new needle and one more color now enters.

She was one of my closest friends—one of those so rare I can count them on one hand. Yesterday we lost her. She was one of those friends you have the deepest heart to hearts with and all those late-night talks where you speak the realest, rawest words.

Another time I'll think about how much and how hard she made all of us laugh and how her bold, vibrant personality and huge heart lit up every room she walked into. And how she lived life more passionately than a dozen people put together. But in this quiet place these past couple days, I've been remembering the quietest stuff.

The doctors told her she had six months. God, in his mercy, gave her a little over four and a half years. Through all the ups and downs of her battling a rare, aggressive cancer, the vast majority of our conversations would naturally gravitate to how good God is. How faithful. How tender. So many bona fide miracles of heart, body, and circumstances came time after time after time within the context of the larger "my grace is sufficient for you," encouraging and sustaining her through this journey and reminding her that God was walking it with her. Reminding her of his goodness and compassion toward her. And awing all of us right along with her.

The gifts always come and go but the giver remains. The gifts we have to hold with open hands. Never harder than when one of those gifts is a much-loved life.

Barely more than a year ago, we got together the morning after the doctors told her they'd no longer operate on her. They ended up operating just once more as palliative care, but it was that first firm "no" at the time that marked a dreaded turning point. That morning started out with the most painful, speechless, shattered tears and with hugs, but by the end of our breakfast full of praying and processing, there she was wanting to pray for our server suffering from a horrible migraine. That was her big heart. She refused to consider another's suffering less than her own, no matter what it was. And by about midway through breakfast and then for the rest of the day, we couldn't stop remarking to each other how light we felt. She was the first one to say it out loud, but I'd been bursting with the same exact thought, the same exact words. It was so potent that we knew it was God doing what only he could do. For hours we each couldn't stop interrupting our conversation to say, "I feel LIGHT. I can't believe how light I feel." This was no high—it was something so quiet, so gentle, but potent.

In the pictures we took that day, we were standing on one end of a bridge. In my gut, I knew this was the start of her walking across one, but there was still that powerful lightness framing that knowledge. She felt God holding on to her that day, and I felt held, too. There was this profound okayness in the midst of circumstances so not okay.

A couple summers ago, we went to a Lyle Lovett concert together, outdoors. We were both in a quiet, contemplative mood. Our conversation that evening was hushed, with lots of space around our words, rather than dense and fervent like many other times. Conversation had been shifting more in that direction for a while now as the present moment grew more precious than anything else that might or might not come. The world was in chaos that week, rocked by violence again, and at the same time she was wondering out loud if she'd still be here a year from then.

During a gospel set, he started singing "I'll Fly Away." She and I sat side by side, quietly singing along together, almost whispering those lines about that short stretch of road left to go before never-ending joy would replace these last weary steps. And it was holy ground. Heaven was so close you could touch it. It was like a cloud of witnesses was singing with us, testifying, so nearly seen in the unseen in that air neither here nor there.

We lingered in our seats after most others were long gone. We two gathered together, God there with us, were still having church. Saying isn't God good, isn't he beautiful. Still asking those questions and talking about what heaven would be like. The smallest taste of it, we would have stayed there all night if security hadn't shooed us out. We walked the long way back to her car.

I've been getting a taste of that same feeling these past weeks. That thin place. And it's been the most distinct taste of intermingled joy and grief that I've ever experienced. I don't know how else to say it other than that there are plenty of tears but, as piercing as they are, the tears feel clean. There's joy in the mix. This sweet friend was one of the biggest gifts God gave so many of us. I miss her terribly already, but there is a consolation so far beyond platitude in knowing where she is right now and that I'll get to see her again. And in the tangible reality of God's presence right in the midst of this loss. Thank you, Jesus.

So much about this is not okay. Cancer is a horror. All she endured for so long. All the times it brought her to her knees. So many loved ones torn away from each other way too soon. So much about this broken world is so unbelievably, excruciatingly hard. But, God.

This isn't about easy answers. It's about being held tight when it hurts the most, the rescue of our hearts over and over, and experiencing peace and hope at the most inexplicable times. He's the reason I find myself singing in the dark. He's the reason she could, too.

•

It was a different kind of cancer that took my dad twenty-two years earlier. Glioblastoma multiforme, an aggressive brain cancer that stole him away just one month after diagnosis.

Within days, this Ph.D. in cognitive psychology couldn't remember the name of the month. Within two weeks, this man who loved few things more than teaching university students could no longer speak and was transferred from hospital to hospice. This force of nature who at fifty-eight could bench press two hundred and fifty pounds and leg press seven hundred could now barely lift his hands.

The sights and sounds of hospice that last week were no sweet movie or television tropes. God must have needed rain barrels instead of bottles to store my tears.

Sometimes we could tell he heard us, but often it seemed he was too far out to sea, closer to another shore than this one.

In that Manoa Valley hospice not long after sunrise, I touched his hand, life no longer coursing through it, skin stretched tight over bone, and couldn't say a word. It was like all the air had been let out of the world.

My grief both before and after that shell-shocked day was the furthest thing from peaceful. Our relationship complex with so much fun, laughter, creativity, and adventure in a disjointed contrast with some darker, more hurtful themes, I was in my twenties and still terribly broken and voiceless, my identity borrowed, not yet fully my own. His presence too powerful, when that tether snapped the centrifugal force sent me flying, spinning for miles, and landing hard and lost. It took a long time to find my footing, my voice, my way, my healthier anchoring.

But even within that context, within a shattered night of prayer, another thin place opened up right there on my knees. It was Easter evening, seven months after his passing. I'd been poring over 1 and 2 Peter and praying for hours. Pouring my heart out to God. In the middle of that it was like heaven opened up and physically touched me. It had never felt so tangibly real, so near. And it struck me that not only was God right there but my dad, by grace made whole and healed and seeing me fully for maybe the first time, was right there with him. It was like God had invited him into that moment for a short time, for both of our sakes.

My brother and I sang "I'll Fly Away" at his memorial service. Joy and grief embroidered together in my spirit. Clashing colors on cloth of grace. Both true. The cloth truer.

•

Easter is almost here again. Not even five months yet since losing my friend. It's a few days into Lent, a few days deep into a month of anticipation and honesty and making some extra space in life for God to move within. And it's a Holy Saturday sort of feeling.

We're no longer midway between the crucifixion and resurrection but midway between the resurrection and the day we get to see Christ's face again in that way most literal. We're in this second advent that spans every day of the year. Midway between the victory and paradise, it's this quiet, even awkward, day of choosing how to spend this day. Waiting to celebrate even as my soul is already swaying to the strains of songs like "Because He Lives."

There is no ceremony, no ritual, to this day, and so I have to choose not to skip forward and miss what it is that today would tell me if I'd only be still enough to listen.

The state of our day to day lives is so clearly this. Jesus is risen, yes! And yet here we are, even still, living some questions and cries and dreams whose answers can only be walked into, one foot after the other.

Between the loss of my dad and the loss of my friend, death hasn't changed but I have. And still I'm changing. As the first Easter after this latest loss approaches, there's a newly discovered wing in my lonely place's caverns that I'm wandering and still getting to know. Crystals shining on the walls. Oh, how I wish she could see it—the colors are just so her, just so amazing. It's big, but I'm not afraid to go deep into it. I'm not alone here.

Life stops now and then, but we have to go on.

Today I don't come to the throne with my list of requests and questions. And on this day of rest, I even set down my doing and trying. In this fallow moment, my soul's inner ear is simply looking for equilibrium. Balancing longing for heaven and this growing intimacy with God right here and now. His kingdom come, his will be done, on earth as it is in heaven. And as it is in me.

> Grace and peace be multiplied to you in the knowledge
> of God and of Jesus our Lord… (2 Pet. 1:2 NASB)

Multiplied. More and more, can you imagine? More grace. More peace. More trust.

More growing. More healing. More freeing.

To get to the heart of Easter and the new life Jesus won for us, we can no more bypass the reality of Holy Saturday than we can skip Good

Friday. All miracle and no process. Jesus was raised, yes. But Peter went through those three days wrestling with having denied Jesus three times out of fear and weakness—the very thing he'd sworn he'd never do.

Is it really this new life we want, a new way of living, step by step with God? Or is it just a cosmic retirement plan that doesn't interfere with us too much? Or spiritual highs we chase one after the other? Or looking good to our colleagues or neighbors?

Jesus rose again and gave us new life. But he leaves us with these lives to live and a continual transformation to undergo. Sanctification, discipleship, surrender as steps to increasing freedom and looking more like him. Lives of waiting for that fullest experience of salvation and yet not waiting at all. Active, present, engaged in the here and now. Doing more than enduring and persevering. God's promises to us tied not just to some future day, but to today. Enabling us to live more fully in the present. Increasingly in Jesus' nature and likeness and sense of companionship. It's himself he promises us. His presence on days just like today.

In the midst of all of these Holy Saturdays that are really our Mondays, our Tuesdays, our everydays, the strains of "Because He Lives" grow louder and echo against every wall. My voice joins in. A cloud of witnesses and I, one choir.

•

1 Cor. 15:55-57, Rev. 21:4

LEAVES

the landscape transformed
these past twenty-four hours
a bed of leaves snow briefly covered
became a sea of brown, gold,
and green
so many leaves fell
before their time
in all their glory
but then who's to say
what time it is
as I walk upon a cloud of
sweetness spent for the sake
of all this beauty
and they remind me of how
God vindicates every bit of life
abandoned to him
so I let go and fall
to my knees again

SHAME

what if they knew
what if they saw
what if they heard
what passed my heart
would judgment crash these gates
with torches flaming

maybe I'll run
from all those eyes
maybe I'll hide
maybe I'll die
a thousand deaths inside

COVERED

These days one comment or photo online can destroy a life. Will one such slip or choice forever define me at some point? What about the words or actions I wish I could take back? My honest mistakes? My worst impulses immediately regretted? The things I've learned only in the messy midst of? The careless words I've spoken in ignorance or thoughtlessness, where it was only through the eyes looking back at me that I understood how they really landed?

Uncovered. Today more than ever, what could be more unsettling?

We cheer when someone blatantly malicious or arrogant falls. When someone who's terrorized or traumatized others with impunity finally gets revealed. When unrepentant evil is brought to light, we heave a sigh of relief and grieve that it didn't happen sooner.

But these days it doesn't take much for a mob to assemble.

And who needs a mob when there's our own internal dialogue. Is it instinctive for all of us, I wonder, when we blow it now and then—do we all have nervous eyes that scan left and right to see who might have noticed? And have all of us at one time or other found our imaginations tallying the possible consequences?

•

On this, the last day of Lent, Jesus' robe caught my attention. The one stripped from him on Golgotha, the Place of the Skull. In front of everybody.

In Eden, the first thing God did after the Fall was to cover us. It took shed blood—an animal slain by his own hands for its fur and skin. The first breath ever stopped. The cost of shame. Cover it with what you can. We know what it's like to hold our breath, trying to keep out the smell of death.

And the last thing we did to Jesus before the cross was to remove his covering. To expose him to shame. And, not only that, but we made a game of it. Casting lots for it, and congratulating. We went so far as to crown him with our curse—those thorns wound round his head to the sound of laughter.

Then Jesus himself became our covering. Not one of matter but of spirit. A covering for our soul that, once received, seals us forever. God's breath of life fills us one more time and makes us brand new. We're born, again.

•

For some reason I woke up feeling a little sorry for myself this morning. I've continued to check myself on whether all this downsizing—not just tackling things but a cluttered mind and heart and schedule—is coming from a healthy place. And, yes, it's coming from a place of passion and curiosity. Maybe it's just that as I get closer to the stripped-down core of me, these uncomfortable feelings naturally come. Either way, I want to deal with this. Rather than just soothing or ignoring this feeling, I want to sit with it and learn what it's about.

This archaeological dig of myself. I'm cooperating with God to remove the dirt around these sleeping bones. At times with shovels and bulldozers but then other times with paintbrushes and Q-tips. Finally, here and there with the breath of God alone, gently blowing away the most delicate layers.

And as I stand here uncovered, the truth of me exposed, God's eyes are compassionate. They're loving. Because it's no longer my lack that he sees; he's looking at what his Son loved so much that he bought back with his life. His life set down and taken back up to show his power and authority beyond where ours stops. His life, our covering.

> Jesus gave them this answer: "Very truly I tell you, the Son can do nothing by himself; he can do only what he sees his Father doing, because whatever the Father does the Son also does." (John 5:19 NIV)

God's own love and mercy. Like Father, like Son.

•

Father God, this world makes it tough to be honest sometimes. People's deepest darkness gets revealed, and the mob says your very need for forgiveness disqualifies you from getting it from us. Then others come clean from the outset, full of repentance, like the mob said the others should have done to win their favor, but the angry gods turn on them, too, saying it's not enough. Saying it'll never be enough, not for them. Their laws have been broken, and there's no coming back from that.

If only I could say these were just some of the most strident among those who don't believe in you who operate like such fundamentalists—their own angry gods, their own harsh laws, hungry for sacrifices enough to satisfy their bloodlust. Trying to separate good and evil as if it doesn't run right through the marrow of each of us. But, Father, even some who call themselves your children join the mob as if they're doing you a favor. As if the fruit of the Spirit are self-righteousness and dogpiling instead of love, joy, peace, patience, kindness, goodness, gentleness, faithfulness, and self-control.

This world increasingly demands a disjointed moral and ideological purity impossible to live up to or fully agree upon. Testifying, in its own broken way, that it understands the extent of the demands of holiness, though it might define it differently.

Father, the price you paid through your Son to free us from the curse of the Law was beyond costly. And your grace and forgiveness remain things that this world struggles to extend without your influence.

> To some who were confident in their own righteousness and looked down on everyone else, Jesus told this parable: "Two men went up to the temple to pray, one a Pharisee and the other a tax collector. The Pharisee stood by himself and prayed: 'God, I thank you that I am not like other people—robbers, evildoers, adulterers—or even like this tax collector. I fast twice a week and give a tenth of all I get.' But the tax collector stood at a distance. He would not even look up to heaven, but beat his breast and said, 'God

have mercy on me, a sinner.' I tell you that this man, rather than the other, went home justified before God. For all those who exalt themselves will be humbled, and those who humble themselves will be exalted." (Luke 18:9-14 NIV)

Father, it's not self-flagellation or humiliation you're looking for like the mob does, it's simple humility. An understanding of the cost of what you cover in us. A fear of—more than anything else—offending you who we love. A fear rooted in gratitude, respect, and awe.

> ...he does not treat us as our sins deserve or repay us according to our iniquities. For as high as the heavens are above the earth, so great is his love for those who fear him; as far as the east is from the west, so far has he removed our transgressions from us. As a father has compassion on his children, so the Lord has compassion on those who fear him... (Ps. 103:10-13 NIV)

Father, thank you. Not only do you forgive when we ask with hearts full of genuine repentance, you never hold it over our heads again. Should there be consequences to face, you walk with us through those full of compassion and love. You love to restore, redeem, and bring beauty and life out of broken things. The artist you are, every possible medium is yours to work with.

It's your goodness, power, and love that enable us to come to you. And to then move forward into something new. You offer us a new page and another when the world considers our story over.

I approach you with both confidence and a realistic take on who I am. In your grace no contradiction, covered as I am.

The wind outside is howling, carrying loosened things down the street. I find myself opening the window. Saying here, take one more thing. Or two. Or three. Blow all night if you want.

Breath of God, blow through my spirit. Carry away from within and around me all that doesn't belong there. All that comes between us.

Uncover me. Then be my covering.

•

Gen. 3:21, Ps. 103:12, Matt. 5:4, Matt. 27:27-31

BLESSED ARE

how blessed are the poor
those with nothing to boast about
except Jesus
even earthly kings have empty hands
before God, and some join
those in rags, nothing but themselves
to offer him
only to find the kingdom gifted

blessed are those who mourn
who see this world for what it is
and themselves, too
in the full light of a holy God
they will be comforted
Jesus wiping tears with his sleeve
from every face
buried against his neck now and then

so blessed are the meek
the ones with strength unexpected
humbly anchored
who can shake the ones rooted in God
what can come against them
their confidence not in themselves
their hands open
they walk the earth, their inheritance

blessed are the hungry
and the thirsty for the holy
silver refined
purified like gold they stand and shine
a cup running over
their empty places filled with grace

there's room for more
of what the sated ones are missing

blessed, the merciful
the ones who give what they most need
remembering
the leniency they themselves receive
the ones whose scales are set
in comparison not to us
but to the One
who himself bought our costly favor

blessed are the pure hearts
those who look in God's direction
seeing, so rare
just because few really want to
so many avoid the
One they love for split motives or
focus, but these
fully live for the eyes that see them

blessed are peacemakers
those who take after their Father
the ones who fight
to reconcile, restore, reinstate
the ones who see all as
mid-story, not ending too soon
the ones who stay
long after pride and hurt walk away

blessed are the abused
the ones for God's sake persecuted
they give their lives
in trade for what they will never lose
the world doesn't get why
so much darkness shines around them

it can't see crowns
on heads bowed, so how can it take them

•

Matt. 5:1-12

PARADISE

Whoever has ears, let them hear
what the Spirit says to the churches.
To the one who is victorious,
I will give the right
to eat from the tree of life,
which is in the paradise of God.
(Rev. 2:7 NIV)

CHERYL VELK

chapter eleven

HOME

MOUNT SAINT HELENS

orange and red
I stood in the middle of the
empty street, staring
at skies supercharged by
ash from three thousand miles away

I was thirteen
and trapped
but, at sunset, freer
than I'd ever felt

the other side of the world
was in reach
it got to me
maybe somehow I got to it, too
maybe it was the one staring

prophesying
beauty for ashes
on display
for miles and miles

SALT + LIGHT

My mother holds onto my arm while we walk across the icy parking lot, and she quotes her own mother, saying, "Race you to the ground."

We laugh, of course, just like we do on our roadtrips, blasting Waylon and Willie.

We live together now. At a certain point you stop caring about the track you think your life is supposed to take, and you decide to live the life that's right in front of you. Each on our own for so long, why not join forces?

What a blessing. The friends who can't imagine such an arrangement, they should be so lucky to come home to such peace and understanding. For the first time in my life, I now come home feeling not just safe but known and loved.

Here now in this space equal parts her and myself, surrounded by some things once used and loved by those no longer around, it feels like grace. She makes chicken soup in the slow cooker, and we talk about real things. We talk about our days and what we're thinking about. We laugh, we nod, we go silent for a bit. As she sits at the table, the photo of her at nineteen or so on the wall, it hangs facing her as if to listen. As if to see who she's become. The woman who no longer dances but lives with that ballerina grace.

Once in a while, I sweep some salt off the counter that she can't see as well anymore, smiling with gratitude because nowadays it's me she sees more clearly. For a long time, it was the reverse. Seeing me would have meant seeing too many other things. But, by God's grace, what used to block vision doesn't anymore. In either of us.

Even just a few years ago, this wouldn't have worked. But again, there are few private earthquakes. And when they hit, a whole lot can happen in a very short time. These things reshape us communally. God's severe mercies like shaking, like fire, like storms.

Last summer we visited New Jersey together for the first time. The place where I grew up. The place where I started using the word "home" more loosely. I'd made a few visits on my own since we moved away, but it'd been ages since the last time.

In the bright green and brick coffee shop in the heart of Princeton, she gestured wide with her arms and said, "It's like all this is healed." Once more I heard my own unspoken thoughts come out of someone else's mouth. Once more God had done something bigger than just me in his compassion and love.

I'd come back expecting the ick to be gone. The thing in me that cringed at the reminders of some really hard years. What I hadn't expected was the reminder and restoration of everything here I'd ever truly loved.

It wasn't this place I'd made peace with. It never needed to make anything up to me. God had brought peace to me that was bigger than this. This door slammed within me had been a door slammed on love. Locked in and buried deep. Lord, I'm tired of locked doors within me.

For the first time in decades I could say "I'm from here" without it sticking in my throat. I could call it home again without it feeling false. For the first time this ugly part of my story felt beautiful.

She took my arm in the summer sun and we crossed the street together.

•

In this crowded world, sometimes it's as if there's nowhere that hasn't already been found. But today every step feels new to me. Somewhere I've never been, like that river no one can step twice in. And yet every step feels like home.

There are different ways we fight for our lives in this modern frontier. Different ways we explore, different things we set our stakes in, assuming we're fast enough and get there first. And yet here I am, placed by God in this space and time. My firm place to stand is not this shifting land but his grace.

Never having owned a place, I think about home and where I'm going.

> Lord, you alone are my portion and my cup; you make
> my lot secure. The boundary lines have fallen for me

in pleasant places; surely I have a delightful inheritance.
(Ps. 16:5-6 NIV)

To be here now, like this, is the last thing I'd ever pictured. But it's beautiful to me. And the story is still being written.

Once again, my season of fruit is intertwined with a season of germinating. All at the same time I am infant, adolescent, and graduate. Even as words have been pouring out in a rush, I'm living new content, new growth, and waiting for new words to form. I stare out of windows like I have from the beginning, wondering where life will carry me next. In cooperation with or in spite of my plans and actions.

There's a leaf clipped to a board on my wall. Last autumn the sight of it there on the ground stopped me mid-stride. Vivid and softer greens, warm orange and gold, and brittle brown, it held all four seasons at once within itself. I know what it must feel like I thought to myself as I picked it up and took it home.

Now winter has claimed the rest of it. As one day winter will claim me. And I read this and long for the day when what will overtake us all is life. Winter is not the end of our story.

> ...On each side of the river stood the tree of life,
> bearing twelve crops of fruit, yielding its fruit every
> month. And the leaves of the tree are for the healing
> of the nations. (Rev. 22:2 NIV)

In paradise, the new heavens and new earth to come, the tree of life will be there, bearing new fruit every month.

Contemplating trees as much as I have over the years and what they have to teach, just now the thought of standing before the tree of life actually caused a stab of alarm and grief. Because even in sunny-year-round places and even here among the evergreens, new life just doesn't come without some dying on the way. If that were the new message, that this is what we'd have to walk through every day—God help us.

But awe and joy equally piercing followed just as quickly. Because I remembered this:

...as it is written: "What no eye has seen, what no ear has heard, and what no human mind has conceived— the things God has prepared for those who love him..." (1 Cor. 2:9 NIV)

I'd been picturing something too much like today. Paradise is still beyond our comprehension.

We're promised that one day we'll be freed from the cycle of life and death—something we think we can picture until specifics like these come up. But one day we'll see what it's like to pass from life to life, blessing to blessing, rather than loss to loss, grave to grave. We'll see seeds not dying but opening their mouths with shouts of praise.

I've often wondered what new metaphors we'll need when eternity comes. When death is done, what will a new creation preach?

And what will become of the warrior hearts when peace finally reigns? When swords are turned into plows' cutting blades and all our fighting is over? What will be our new questions and adventures?

More than a few times I've tried to imagine a brand new periodic table of elements or spectrum of color. But even that, I know, is thinking too small. The opportunities for discovery will never run out. And we won't tire of it all like we sometimes do now.

This tree with its new fruit each month, whatever else it is or represents, hints of a future of rhythms and process and development but death no longer in the equation. Out of all the things we can't yet imagine, that one is toward the top of my list.

Even now, how is it that my greatest losses have come hand in hand with blessings and beginnings and mysteries that fill my life to overflowing? I couldn't always say that.

Tastes of your kingdom, Lord. Tastes of a forever home to come.

Just we two, my mother and I at this table, we talk about heaven. We talk about paradise. We talk about seeing Jesus return, just like he said he would. We talk about how all things will finally be made right, and how we're looking forward to bodies that don't hurt or break down anymore.

We talk about how good this feels right here, right now. The grace that finds us in this place after such long, winding stories. How good God is. How kind, how faithful. We talk about how nothing's worth more than spending our lives with and for him.

These are special days. Still, there's no mistaking this for our final destination. We stand in church side by side, hands raised, singing come, Lord.

Come quickly. As quickly as you can.

•

Matt. 5:13-16, John 14:3, Rev. 12:11

I HAVE TO PRAISE YOU

My heart must sing
'cause words are not enough
I have to dance
when your mercy comes
I have to fall on my knees
when chains break free
I have to praise you

I have to climb
when you tell me to stand
I have to hope
when your strength is all I have
I have to walk straight ahead
though you're all I can see
I have to praise you

Lord, all I am
needs everything you are
All I have done
has seen your scars
I have to sing holy, holy
my Lord God Almighty
I have to praise you

You know I am the least of these
still you called me by my name
Your glory fills gold vessels
the same as it fills clay
Everything I am is reaching
out to hold you tight
and to be held by you
I have to praise you
I have to praise you

LOSS + GAIN

what profit
could ever it be
to gain the world
in its entirety
and lose your soul
forever

what loss
could ever it be
to lose the world
in all ways worth mentioning
and gain this King
forever

•

Mark 8:36-37

PRESENCE

What's the hardest "no" you ever said? What about the healthiest? What made it hard? What made it crazy to do otherwise?

No wasn't a word that used to come easily to me. To cost anyone anything—a hard feeling, time, effort, inconvenience—was on the terrifying side. If a friend, foe, or romantic interest was upset with me, even if the logic of the accusation was nonsensical to the point of bad comedy, the button their anger or hurt pushed in me was that it was my responsibility to fix this. To be their fix. That the internal sacrifice of self-respect or peace was the price I had to pay for a return to relational safety.

Years after getting over that nonsense, which was anything but easy, a cute neighbor moved in a couple doors down. There were a few fleeting conversations and smiles in passing. But I lived close enough to see the comings and goings of him and his women, so I just shrugged and knew it was more of the same.

Over Christmas while he was gone, I picked up his newspaper, and to thank me he left a bottle of wine. How classy and nice, right? A few days later, though, he was back at my door. After a minute of it sinking in that he'd really just asked for what he'd asked for—a New Year's kiss, right then and there, and something cringey and bizarre about claiming his rights as a neighbor—I smiled and tried not to laugh as I politely declined the proposition.

Not one date, much less last names or more than a one-minute conversation. Intimacy without relationship—just not my style. With a seven-dollar bottle of wine, he'd tried to buy something that wasn't for sale.

As I shut the door and turned away, I erupted into laughter. What was that? Was he out of his gourd? And look at me, feeling so free after all my mental gymnastics once upon a time.

Thankfully, in this case, a little awkwardness was the only aftermath to deal with. Friends, family, flirters, and adversaries can ask a lot, and can have intense reactions to our answers when they're not the ones they want. You have to be able to withstand those accusations when you know what does and doesn't align with your ground rules.

Any parent standing firm as their kid shouts, "It's not fair! I hate you!" will know what I'm talking about.

It was Psalm 5 that came up on the heels of all this.

> But I, by your great love, can come into your house; in reverence I bow down toward your holy temple. (Ps. 5:7 NIV)

> But let all who take refuge in you be glad; let them ever sing for joy. Spread protection over them, that those who love your name may rejoice in you. Surely, Lord, you bless the righteous; you surround them with your favor as with a shield. (Ps. 5:11-12 NIV)

House. Refuge. Protection. Shield.

It got me reflecting on how not everyone gets to claim God's home as their own. Just like with Mr. Smooth, we spoke at the door, but he couldn't just charge into my inner space as if it belonged to him. God loves all, Jesus conquered death and bridged the way to the Father and no one is left out of that invitation, but there's still that threshold that only those who enter into relationship with him can cross.

The sanity and safety of being able to close out that person who was coming to me in an inappropriate way felt healthy, not selfish or cruel.

The shelter of God's home is safe and private, set apart. Not just under a wing, but behind a solid door of sorts.

Heaven is the place where God dwells. His most intimate home. There are new heavens and earth coming when that here-and-there distinction will be removed, but for now it's that place we can't see. When we get to its door the one and only question that matters will be, "Do you know the host?"

•

The Holy of Holies was the most sacred place in the temple, enclosed by a curtain that was thirty feet high, heavy and thick. Only the high priest could go within, and only once a year on the Day of Atonement. So many purification rituals, so much caution, to be in God's presence for even just a moment. It's still hard for me to get my head around the degree of purity and holiness, but Eden and the cross remind me of what had been lost. To think we'd once walked there freely.

> And when Jesus had cried out again in a loud voice, he gave up his spirit. At that moment the curtain of the temple was torn in two from top to bottom. The earth shook, the rocks split. (Matt. 27:50-51 NIV)

Torn from top to bottom. The curtain around the Holy of Holies. Why didn't it turn to ash? Or unravel? Or drop from shattered clasps? Torn—why that?

Back when we had phone books, and back when they were still four or five inches thick, my dad was strong enough to tear them in half with his bare hands. Every muscle was involved, and there was that set to his chin. With one yank, the whole thing was rent.

Have you ever torn a photo in half rather than just throwing it away? What were you trying to say?

Put both of these things together, and you've got this curtain. To tear something this big is to involve spirit in a physical act of destruction. It's emotional.

I picture God, the split second his Son's suffering ended and our full debt was paid, taking that thick curtain, that veil, and with one yank destroying what had separated us from his most intimate presence. The words on his heart: It was never supposed to be this way.

•

The kingdom is near. I'm hearing that softly this week and hearing the immediacy rather than somedayness of it. The kingdom is near, now. The kingdom is as near as the song in my ear. As near as the breath in this body.

Father God, you're my home. Not just a place I'm waiting to get to, but a place I already have. I'm overcome by your love that invites, welcomes, covers, protects. All these years you've been my shelter and strength. My wisdom, my comfort, the light unto my path. In your presence I've laughed until I've cried and cried until I've laughed.

One day we'll be face to face in a more literal sense. One day faith will become sight, and so much more will fall away.

Father, it's not yet the full kingdom reality. It's not yet the day we'll be freed from all we deal with in this life. But it's a type of fullness that you'd have us walk in. More and more, and daily.

Father God, I can never earn what you have for me. It's all grace. And yet I can resist or welcome what you have for me. I can resist you or say yes from moment to moment. I can hold fast to ego or control or the past, or I can hold fast to you.

I need your help, though. I need your courage, strength, and peace to let you into these places in me. Move in power within my surrender. How else will your kingdom come in me and among us? Your fully functioning body, participating in your will and living out your heart in this world.

I want to increasingly know what it means to walk in your wisdom, peace, and strength rather than my own. To be a deeply rooted tree that strong winds can't shake.

I do sometimes wonder about heaven. What life will be like after this part of the story. What new metaphors we'll need. The best I can ever do is picture idealized versions of now. But like your Word says, it's beyond our comprehension.

What matters right now, what's here for me to live out, is the commonality of the kingdom. Both now and forever, the kingdom is the kingdom. Imperfectly though we walk it out, we're its residents already. Father, your will be done here as it is in heaven. Help us learn what it means to move in that direction together.

I am right here, right now. Homesick for that day, that state, but at the same time more present to the here and now and what you're doing. This moment is more crucial, more relevant. More rich, not less. This is an active kind of waiting.

Embers have been glowing and popping in me as I stir up these thoughts. Right here, right now. The kingdom. The King. Your reign. Your peace.

Where am I in my lonely place? Lying in the grass beneath leaves of the tree of life, its branches stretched out like a canopy. At rest.

•

Isa. 25:8, Isa. 65:17, John 14:2-4, Rom. 5:1, Rom. 8:15, 1 Cor. 2:9

GATHERED

every tribe, tongue and nation
the blessed of every age
will sing their song
will dance their dance
before the Lamb
before the King

children will dance with elders
the strong will sing with the weak
with abandon
with hearts of peace
before the Lamb
before the King

so come, Lord, come Son of Man
hear our praise
I can't wait to see your face
come again, Lord, just as you planned
may your will be done in my heart
and in this place

•

Rev. 7:9

CHERYL VELK

chapter twelve

FREEDOM

CHERYL VELK

GREEN

sleeping-red beating
dreaming-grey stealing away
seeing-blue brimming
at waves of green rolling ahead

further from the shore
further than I've ever been before
past an ancient garden graveyard
roads there long grown over
even maps have faded and a
child's hand laughing pulled me away

no markers to set bearings by
nothing but this sky
filling my lungs like they've
never tasted air before
or felt this alive

breath given these sails
flooded soul amazed
this green could make a heart break
too small to hold this grace

SHIFTING + STANDING

trying to name this shift
into a new way of being...
the words are hiding
but I'm looking

I more fully trust, yet
struggle still for footing against
waves assaulting and
battering shore

battering me

trying to get me to
disavow the peace given me
spiked with truth, the
lies reach full din

all of that, it can still
steal my footing for a moment
only I tend to
rise laughing now

laughing and drenched

something like laughter lifts
me up and steadies me again
what I'm standing on
is so solid

FAITHFUL

Light plays across sagebrush, prairie grass, and earth, nothing but blue skies and painted clouds above for miles in every direction, and the country feels big again. We're somewhere between Muddy Gap and Laramie, making our way north to a spot we'd been aching to get back to for years.

There's a family connection to Yellowstone National Park. My mother's father worked there with the Civilian Conservation Corps in the 1930s, so that particular park has always felt a little more like "ours" than any other. In his small, green Haynes Guide on a shelf at home, signed by friends, his tentmate describes him as staunch and laconic and compares him to Jim Bridger. At heart, our dear engineer was also an explorer. My mother and I share a few memories of him as we drive.

We arrive in Jackson Hole, check in, and unpack. The place has been newly remodeled and still smells like sawdust. It's the last day of my forties, and after the long drive my spirit links my body's tiredness to the past fifty years. But it's a good kind of tired. I've arrived somewhere worth reaching.

The next morning, we get an early start. We make it to Old Faithful and no one else is around. It's partially surrounded at a safe distance by a crescent of metal benches. They're all empty at this chilly, early hour. We have our pick of seats, and I choose one that's familiar.

A month or so ago, I finally looked through some old photos transferred from slides to digital a year or two earlier. I'd been avoiding them because they cover a time of life I don't enjoy remembering. Our carefree, goofy smiles and hamming-it-up poses had started to shift around that time. Expressions had turned hurting and weighed down, and body language had turned self-conscious and awkward. But partway through the collection, I struck gold. Pictures of one of our trips to Old Faithful from exactly forty years ago. Tears sprang to my eyes, wishing I could reach back and tell ten-year-old me that everything was going to be all right. A wave of gratitude surged through me, and I spent all evening praising God for his faithfulness. He'd rescued me.

It's spring now. Elsewhere some days are starting to pass for summer, but here in Yellowstone we need our coats and gloves. Getting colder by the minute as we wait patiently on this bench, it's about forty-five minutes before others begin to join us. They'd checked the visitor center's sign for the next estimated time of eruption; we hadn't.

I could have checked, but the act of waiting in this open-ended way is too big a part of the prayer flowing through me, along with song after song of praise, and joyful memories of all God has done.

People come from all over the world to see this geyser in action, so remarkable is its constancy. This morning I don't need, or even want, to know when it will erupt. It's enough to know that it will. Waiting for this hour or so I've been testifying in my spirit: yes, this is just what life is like now. Songs of praise and gratitude welling up in me as I wait with and for our faithful God.

My younger self sat in this same exact seat forty years earlier. And today, she and I are bound together like covers of a book about God's faithfulness. I'm here to tell him "thank you" for every single page.

•

Father God, it's no secret that I'm still a work in progress. I still have my moments and spend some harder days and nights with you at Gethsemane and Golgotha. And I'm still subject to every season. This world is bound to keep razing me down to my foundations.

But this was never about self-actualization. And, I'm finding, it wasn't even about the circumstances I'd dreamed would wrap up so neatly.

No, this has had more to do with you and my prayer to trust you. And how you've woven your answer into the fabric of me over a lifetime.

In you, Lord, I'm free. Once and for all so long ago now, but every day experienced more deeply. It's not so much about my being more or less than I was, but about the strengthened knowledge that every time I open my clenched hands in your presence, I find them far from empty.

Here again, Lord, are my open hands. Never stop taking them in yours.

•

Ps. 18:1-19, Ps. 25:3-5, Ps. 27:14, Ps. 33:20-22, Is. 40:30-31

NO CONTRADICTION

I can do all things in your strength
I can do nothing without you
I am poor, I am rich
I am strong, I am weak

Child of God yet here on my knees
calling you Lord of my life
Before your throne who can stand—
but I draw near with confidence

You're my beginning
You're my destination
You're in every breath and step that I take

I'm part, not the whole
yet in fullness I go
In boldness and humility, in your name

INSPIRATION

whisper music language
like a thousand chanting petals

when silent songs rising within
smell like rain to the soul

and those words not yet born
speak of storms and dreams and life to come

don't be afraid when you look up
and see them all start to fall

drink it in and tend to the green things
that follow the thunder

and sing again, fearless
and full of wonder

SPACE

loss makes me quiet
then again so does victory
so much to take in
so much space that
wasn't there yesterday

SEA CREATURE

holding my breath
as the water rises
I remember dreams as a child
underwater, breathing

is this what it feels like
when love throws itself down
over chasms, a bridge, and
never feels certain footsteps
cross on its back

how can love stand it

I call out to the Overcomer
and he overcomes me again with
his strength and kindness, and
his breath of life fills me again

I close my eyes as
sea creatures sing hallelujah

•

Ps. 148:7

DOORS + LIGHT

I'd never seen a bird weep before.

The bird wasn't a baby and it wasn't an adult. It was a small child. Or maybe, in bird years, more like a teen. It must have come up from the woods bordering the far side of the parking garage. There all three levels of it were open to the wilder world, not quite crowded out by all man had made. The rooftop, itself a parking lot, was flush with the street and the tree-lined sidewalk. The view there was concrete and asphalt meeting sky, but still the small glass room at the top of the stairwell was one of the few visual clues that we were on a hill at all, much less one that big. It just didn't feel like one.

The air was crisp that first day of autumn after the surprise snow the day before, and I'd gone out for lunch to enjoy it. This garage wasn't where I parked, it was just my shortcut between the office and a Greek salad. Walking back now in not too much of a hurry, as I climbed the last flight of stairs the sound hit my ears. I hesitated a bit, trying to picture what was up there first. A few cautious steps later, I saw it and stopped.

A bird was darting across the room, desperately throwing itself against the windows, the impact throwing it back on the concrete landing. A frenzied ball rolling, clawing the air and ground, it kept scrambling back up to do it again. And again. And again. Exhausted but frantic, its entire body was heaving with its gasping chirps. I don't know how else to describe the sounds it was making except to say that it was weeping. Gasping and weeping uncontrollably.

A silent cry of my own welled up and stuck in my throat. After several more steps to the top, I now stood there just a couple feet away from it, sharing that space. Bearing witness. And I wanted to weep with it. And fight for it. Even more so because it was a little too familiar. I knew what it felt like.

Carefully moving to the door, I pushed it open just as two men approached. "There's a baby bird trapped in there," I said, not sure what to call an adolescent bird not quite grown.

"Yeah, we saw that!"

I told them I was just going to stand there awhile with the door open to see if it would fly out.

Something softened in them like a dove had landed in their spirits, and in silent agreement they went in. Their calm hearts entered, and they held out their arms, walking with legs wide and slowly turning to fill and still the space. It was as if they carried quietness like a physical property you could measure with the right kind of instrument, adding it to the room. The bird kept tumbling and darting against the windows, around and in between them. But then its attention finally shifted with the new obstacles in the way—finally ones it could see—and it tried a new direction. Not toward the door, but to the darkest part of the room. It landed on the dingy ledge above the turn of the stairs at the opposite end. Its first moment of shaking stillness since this all began.

After a patient pause, one of them began to move toward it as I stood further off to the side of the door that I still held open. I said, "Try to scare it this way." That didn't come out how I meant—none of us wanted to scare it, we just knew it was scared.

In the quivering quiet, the creature soon became transfixed by the open doorway straight ahead. Was it air? Was it more of that wall it couldn't see? Wondering, fearing, hoping. Its sides heaving in and out, breathing deep but steady now with gathering strength. The stillness was helping it to see a new possibility.

The man was almost to the ledge now, and he raised his index finger like a perch, moving it closer and closer to the bird's feet, slow and steady as a glacier. And then, the moment his finger could go no further without touching it, like an arrow from a bow stretched to its limit the bird soared straight through into the open air. Into freedom.

Holy.

We all just stood there a minute, struck mute by awe and wonder. Smiling at each other, and to ourselves, watching it go. Lost in thought and at a loss for words.

Eventually we nodded to each other with a smile and a little wave, still unable to break the silence, and quietly went our opposite directions.

•

I've thought a lot about that day in the years since then. Remembering walking back to my desk shining, or so it felt, from the holiness of the ground we'd found ourselves on. Joy and praise to God flooding, full force, through me. The whole scene replaying and revealing to me something about who and how I want to be in loving those around me when it comes to certain things. Simply holding a door open and getting out of the way. And knowing it's not all me.

But also remembering one other thing. The quiet thing I saw but then didn't say. Hiding it away in me to rise like bread in its own timing. Something familiar and crystal clear to my spirit but my head still trying to wrap itself around it.

That bird, after soaring about fifty feet, ended its high arc in the shelter of the back tire of a parked truck. In seconds it had beelined for the nearest dark place and landed there, its body still billowing in and out with a hundred different undulating thoughts and emotions. Still shaking from the courage it had taken to trust and from the adrenalin of the fight. Needing to get its bearings in this completely unfamiliar place.

Who knows how long it stayed there. I didn't want to walk away but knew it was necessary. Despite how enraptured I remained, that part haunted me. It had been a completely different day for that bird and for the rest of us who'd been there.

My own soaring arc into a new level of freedom this year ended in what felt like seconds. I'd had just a couple months on my own mountaintop before the script was flipped and, to be honest, I felt a little ripped off. Some of the greatest peace, joy, fun, and excitement I'd ever known, feeling like I'd been released into a whole new level of blessing and living, had been followed so closely by one of the most intense few months ever of battle and struggle. It was like the whole world had erupted all at once around me. I felt dogpiled by trauma. Others' and my own. Lives were on the line, and so were bodies and futures and hearts.

I had a sneaking suspicion that, in the unseen, a great battle had broken out. Part of that story so much bigger than our own. And instead of crumbling, I found myself praying in total confidence and surrender, "Lord, nothing's ever going to steal your praise from my lips. No matter what comes." Over and over.

Not that long ago my prayer might have been, "God, where are you?" This time that thought didn't even come up.

By Thanksgiving everything had shifted more or less all at once. Surveying the battlefield, one life was saved and one life was lost. The barrage of goodbyes had stopped. A series of medical complications ended, and the road seemed to be simplifying and easing up, though there remained things to follow up on. And joy and peace overtook the land in me again and started bubbling up from the unlikeliest places. Even in the face of the losses still being grieved.

The surge of freedom that followed all of that came more gently than the one this spring. In spring a tsunami of release, and this autumn more like a change of seasons. I can't pinpoint the moment things changed, there were just some random moments when it started to dawn on me that a shift had already begun. And the distinct awareness of it is lingering. No high, but a new way of being.

So now I've come back to that same clearing where, years ago, I first stopped in that trembling way and called out for help. That center of my lonely place it had taken so long to get to in the first place. And I'm struck by the contrast. Struck by the stillness within me. And struck by the bigness of this space both in and around me and of the question that keeps repeating: Now what?

I'd stepped into new life in Jesus when I was five, and so in one sense I've always been walking in freedom. Born again, saved, all those expressions we use that mean that moment we say "Jesus is Lord" and are indwelled by the Holy Spirit. Saved, above all other things, from life without him. But despite my best intentions, it had taken years to shift from my way of doing and thinking about things to God's way to a degree that broke the chains in me. To untangle what the world and my own choices and nature had fashioned within me. To reveal the lies and rewrite the narratives. And to begin to see what God intended when he rolled up his sleeves in answer to my bended knee. It took a while for me to get—

really get—how he saw me because for too long my perception of all the eyes physically in front of me had carried all the weight.

I'll always be a work in progress, but today I'm on the other side of a mountain I'd spent my whole life climbing. One I often wondered if I'd die on, unable to imagine ever cresting it.

But I did. And here I am back in this clearing. Breathing easy. Calm. Quiet. And a little disoriented—one more thing I didn't expect. It might look like street level to everyone else, but here—right down here—is a summit I've just now reached and had to fight my way to get to. People walk around like it's ordinary, but to me it's the edges of heaven.

•

Jesus, yes, it's you I need to talk to right now. I've been thinking about you in this place. After the cross, after your depths of suffering, you returned to the fullness of your glory and the right hand of your Father. But you didn't waste a moment before entering right back into our labor. Your own suffering ended but you turned right around to continue faithfully entering into ours. Interceding for us. You're still giving your life away. And I never quite realized just how divine that part of your story is. And what a miracle it is when people reflect that aspect of you. When I see you walking it out in them. It makes a lot of sense theoretically until you get a taste of what they're giving up and understand the cost.

Me, I wanted to hear the snap of a finish line tape and see what it would feel like to know that kind of relief. And for a couple months, in concentrated form, you gave me that powerful, joyful taste.

But my own challenges, those were still there, just waiting for me to reengage with them. The changes in my heart, mind, and spirit had not exempted me.

And, actually more pressing, right back beside me were those friends still dealing with their own challenges and heartaches and asking you their own questions. And being patient and present with them now was suddenly a whole lot harder. It started costing something new. Like remembering some things and revisiting some places it would have been so much easier not to.

Savior, Lord, I didn't come out of this with all-purpose, pat answers to hand out like teaspoonfuls of verbal elixir. I came out of all of this with you. My own answers from you had not come through words alone, they'd come the long way. Layer by layer. Revelation by revelation. Step by step. Friends there beside me in your name, encouraging, exhorting, interceding, bearing witness, standing vigil, listening. Some things take so much more than telling.

It's not that I didn't have my own fresh round of questions and mysteries to explore. It's not that you weren't already leading me forward and stretching me again. I just wasn't quite ready to accept that the long road would take revisiting, much less so quickly. My own challenges and my new questions, I could distract myself from those for a short time, to a degree—but not theirs. Caring takes surrender when it cuts that close to home. Through it, you were asking me to return to the road. Theirs. Mine. Ours.

In a last-ditch attempt to stay in that place of comfort and rest, I didn't just shelve my own harder stuff for as long as I could. I wanted to offer others something to fast-forward them through their individual battles and varied questions—something that had hurt me when subjected to it by others. I wanted to provide easy outs from the internal wrestling matches playing out in front of me. I wanted all of us at a place of forward motion and experiencing companionship with you. As if all it takes in us and in the body of Christ is a little duct tape and WD-40. And once in a while a stab of anger or frustration would hit. Sure, it had taken me years to internalize so many things repeated to me over and over, but I suddenly hated that once wasn't enough with the same words spoken to others.

I knew better. And I knew I knew better. I knew full well that it takes more than information. It often takes time for thoughts to sink in and for dots to connect. Or for tools, strategies, and patterns to be set down or kick in. Or for healing or repentance to happen. It wasn't a matter of knowledge; it was a matter of my tired heart's will.

I hadn't expected that. The need to grieve my return to the road and resume walking with others at paces just as one-step-at-a-time as ever.

Never expected that one at all. It's not who I thought I was. Not after all of this.

All this was easier before my taste of release and relief. Before that taste of heaven. Before finding my fuller hope, trust, and freedom in you. Lord, it was painful to give up a measure of hard-won comfort and have fresh patience with others' burdens, lagging steps, and detours.

It took a couple months of this complaint to recognize the new lagging steps and detours of my own for what they were.

Lord, one morning after another frustrating encounter, I was finally ready to hear it and you rocked me to my core: What I'd been complaining to you about was a road you knew all too well. It's a road you chose and have been on with me from the beginning. And in my resistance to all this, I'd been avoiding imitating you. Avoiding the very thing you did and never stop doing. Every day, from the other side of the cross, the other side of the resurrection, you're still laying down your life for us. This is what your freedom looks like. This is how you spend it. On your bride. On us. And on those who may still come to know you—those whose names you're calling, even now.

And right there, right then, my clenched hands opened one more time.

Jesus, you didn't hand me the master key when you unlocked so many chambers of my puzzle-box heart. That's still in your possession. And each and every heart I come in contact with is its own riddle. Forgive me for even trying to jimmy open what you designed, and life and choices have worked together to fill. I thought it was out of love, but love is patient and I wasn't. Help me to honor the mystery each and every person is and must make their way through.

It's a few months later now. And once again, those I encourage, or pray for, or pass on something to that took me far too long to learn myself, they're among my own encouragers, intercessors, and teachers. Still. Just like before. Plenty of things remain for me—just like them—to wrestle with, repent of, learn, step into, and gather courage for. And I'm fooling myself if I think there aren't other chambers in me that still need opening so your light can fill them. And new arrows still fly and hit their targets on the daily. We'll never stop needing each other. Needing each other to be your hands, feet, and arms in our lives. And we'll never stop needing to lift our prayers and praise to you together.

When I finally set down this pen tonight, this story won't be over. And I know you didn't just bring me to this place for what I'd produce. You brought me to this place to truly live. With you and in you. I'll have to get up tomorrow and move forward.

I know you've got some of your own plans for me to step into. That doesn't make me grand, it just makes me yours. Part of your body. Part of what you're doing. But I'm also hearing you ask, "What do you want to do?" And I don't mind saying it's freaking me out a little. I've been mountain climbing for most of my life. It's taken most of my strength, energy, and time. And despite all the changes and chances and adventures that came before, the question feels new.

I'm back on the road now. A beginner rather than the finished thing I might have felt like for five seconds in that celebratory rush. Humbled, but again saying, "Okay." And instead of a finish line that I just about had to drag myself across, or a desperate yes said at the end of myself, this time this feels more like ribbon and tissue paper falling away from a present in my hands.

A little like that bird hiding in the shade of that truck's tire, I'm still getting my bearings and trying to figure out what this new chapter will even look like. But it's okay to not be able to picture it yet. With your help I'll figure it out. Step by step with you, the author and finisher of our faith.

The question that's felt so big, in a nutshell, is what will I do with my freedom. Lord, if I haven't yet said it this clearly, I give it back to you. It's one more way I want to look a little more like you.

•

John 1:1-18, 2 Cor. 1:3-4, Eph. 1:17-23, Eph. 2:10, Eph. 2:17-22, Heb. 12:1-2

BRIDGE

for years now I've felt like
I live on a bridge
a keeper, an escort
a lantern holder
I accompany people across it, but
my home is on it
neither here nor there
I am liminal space
God my here
God my there
telling me not to worry
about the length and breadth
of my boundaries
the wood worn with passings
is beautiful

EPILOGUE

Together, these songs sung in gardens are my love letter to God. My reason for the hope within me. It's my story woven into his and into him. It's his story woven into mine and into me.

I'd wanted to publish this before the start of spring. Before Lent and Easter. Valentine's Day, to be exact.

As that date and the following cluster of markers all began to pass out of reach one by one, I rode alternating waves of peace and perplexity through delays beyond my control, wondering what they were about.

Meanwhile, news accounts were increasing around the globe of an approaching threat. A patch of black ice that would make its way under the feet of us all by the time it was through. A trial that was about to take everyone to their own lonely place.

A pandemic, of all things. COVID-19.

Health isn't its only casualty; it's hit industries, livelihoods, and schools like an earthquake. And that's just the short list.

You'd think that would have been enough, but the year was just getting started. Political polarization. Extremism. Events freshly revealing both how far we've come and how far we've yet to go on the subject of race. A whole world both divided and united in all manner of upheaval. Ugliness and beauty both in the sharpest of relief. And we're still just halfway through the year.

What's next, we all wonder. By this time next year, who and how and where will we all be? With ourselves, with God, with each other. No matter where anyone's coming from, towering question marks stand before every one of us.

It's summer now and this book is finally moving forward again. The timing of its release not mine, but God's. And it seems that what he's had in mind is more of a nondescript Holy Saturday kind of a day. Closer to the thirty-year anniversary of the day I prayed that prayer, "God, help me trust you." A day when I had no idea what was coming next and something better was almost too much to hope for. A day when I desperately wanted and needed to know God's heart, presence, and trustworthiness right in the middle of pain, fear, confusion, messiness, aloneness, loss, and trial.

Even just four months ago, I was still wondering how many or how few could relate to any of that. Not anymore.

For some this time is agony and for some it's rest. For some it's grounding and for some it's unmooring. For some it's resetting and for some it's chaos. For some it's prison and for some it's freedom. For some it's inconvenience and for some it's life and death. But I don't know a single person exempt from a measure of loss or challenge. So many plans are delayed or abandoned. So much is changing. So much is uncertain.

Some days it's hard to know what to pray for, so diverse and great are the needs. So, on those days my prayers turn to praise. I just remember, and I sing songs like "Great Is Thy Faithfulness," "It Is Well," and "Amazing Grace." I head to my lonely place's gardens, and to those of my friends, and I catch glimpses of new things growing. In and between and around us. Something beautiful and new is happening, even here, even now. Even though I don't have the vantage point to see it in full. And sometimes I hear footsteps in the cool of the day, walking among us.

I ask, "Are you the Gardener?" And he says, "Yes. Yes, I am."

It took about a month into pandemic lockdown life for the thought to occur to me. Maybe this isn't just my love letter to God; maybe, more than even that, it's a reminder of his love letters to me. Letters I still need to reread. Themes that have layers left to go in me.

Such a mystery. My greatest offerings to God revealed as things he first gave to me.

To all who've made it to this last page and to those still on the way, may the Lord bless and keep you. May he make his face shine upon you and be gracious to you. May he turn his face toward you and give you his peace. May he give you a new song, and may you find your voice and sing.

•

Ps. 46:1-3, Num. 6:24-26

ACKNOWLEDGEMENTS

Above all, I'm thankful for the ways in which God, through his Son, has made himself known to me. For his faithfulness and goodness. For his giving me a song to sing.

Do you know what grace it is for family to bless your desire to be real and tell some harder truths? I'll always be grateful for their support and trust as I take this leap. Special thanks to my mother, Vera Velk, for her unwavering encouragement.

Maryann Eberle's sharp eyes, generosity, honesty, and questions were all so invaluable when I handed her the first draft—and the next, and the next. A writer/editor and my closest friend and confidante since childhood, what a treasure she's been on so many levels.

The last five months of her life, Danielle "Bess" Vannice was one of just a few people who knew I was writing this book. She read the first pages, and we often talked about the subject matter. She knew, too, that some of this was going to be about her. The less likely it became that she'd get to read the ending, the more passionately she prayed over my words. What a gift she was to so many of us and, in so many ways, still is.

I was grateful for Kelly Korak long before this book's cover design, which she so lovingly crafted. How priceless her friendship was through many of the transformational years I write about in here, with her deep faith, compassion, truth telling, and sense of humor.

There are so many others who've impacted my story more than they know. Especially those among God's family, Christ's body, his church, which took me far too long to start finding a real place in. Not just within sanctuary walls but beyond them, living life together. By God's artistry and grace, my life would not be the same without a single one of them.

Writing is such a solitary process. But line after line, so many faces come to mind. What life exponential, here in this rich ecosystem of community where such wild things grow.

ABOUT THE AUTHOR

Cheryl Velk is a contemplative in a noisy world, with a heart for unity in Christ's church. She works in the corporate world, but it wasn't until she shifted away from roles focused so fully on writing, editing, and design that her own writing resurfaced and began to develop with greater momentum. She's traveled the long way through life by way of Illinois, California, New Jersey, Colorado, New Mexico, Hawaii, and Johnston Atoll, though the greatest mileage has been internal. These days she's back out west, with those mountains and seasons she loves so much.

Made in the USA
Columbia, SC
24 August 2020